ActionScript for Flash MX
Pocket Reference

Colin Moock

Beijing · Cambridge · Farnham · Köln · Paris · Sebastopol · Taipei · Tokyo

ActionScript for Flash MX Pocket Reference
by Colin Moock

Copyright © 2003 O'Reilly & Associates, Inc. All rights reserved.
Printed in the United States of America.

Published by O'Reilly & Associates, Inc., 1005 Gravenstein Highway North,
Sebastopol, CA 95472.

Editor:	Bruce Epstein
Production Editor:	Emily Quill
Cover Designer:	Emma Colby
Interior Designer:	David Futato

Printing History:

March 2003:	First Edition.

0-596-00514-8
[C]

Contents

ActionScript for Flash MX Pocket Reference

Introduction

ActionScript is Macromedia Flash's scripting language, used to create everything from graphic user interfaces and games to sound sequencers and animated screensavers. Syntactically, ActionScript is nearly identical to JavaScript (both are based on the ECMA-262 specification), but it is tailored to Flash content rather than HTML content. ActionScript also resembles Java and C++, using many of the same statements, operators, and punctuation found in those languages. ActionScript supports both procedural and object-oriented programming or any mix of the two.

This book provides "just the facts" coverage of ActionScript for Flash MX (the sixth version of the software). Differences from ActionScript for Flash 5 (the first official version of ActionScript) are covered at *http://www.moock.org/webdesign/lectures/newInMX/*. For exhaustive coverage of ActionScript, consult O'Reilly's *ActionScript for Flash MX: The Definitive Guide*.

Authoring ActionScript Code

All code in a Flash document (a *.fla* file) must be attached to either a keyframe on the timeline, or a button or movie clip on the Stage.

To attach code to a keyframe:

1. Select the keyframe in the timeline (by clicking it)
2. Open the Actions panel (Window → Actions or F9)
3. Add the desired code to the right side of the panel (called the Script pane)

NOTE

The Actions panel has two different modes of operation, Normal Mode (menu-driven code creation) and Expert Mode (manual typing). To change the mode, use the pop-up Options menu in the upper-right corner of the panel, as shown in Figure 1.

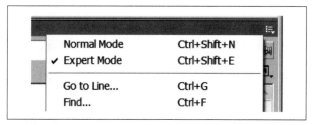

Figure 1. Setting the Actions panel to Expert Mode

During playback, Flash executes the code on a keyframe before displaying the contents of that frame (allowing the code to manipulate elements on the Stage before they are displayed). To add a new keyframe to a timeline, select a frame in the timeline and choose Insert → Keyframe.

To attach code to a button or movie clip:

1. Select the button or movie clip on the Stage
2. Open the Actions panel
3. Add the desired code to the right side of the panel

Code attached to buttons or movie clips must be contained within *event handlers*, which determine when the code

---

should execute at runtime. For example, to invoke the function *submitForm()* when a button is clicked, attach the following code to the button:

```
on (release) {
  submitForm();
}
```

Similarly, to reposition a movie clip five pixels to the left as the playhead advances through the timeline (i.e., once for every tick of the frame rate), attach the following code to the clip:

```
onClipEvent (enterFrame) {
  this._x -= 5;
}
```

For information on button and movie clip events, see "Event Handling."

Outputting Debug Messages

The Flash authoring tool provides a "Test Movie" mode (Control → Test Movie), which is used to compile a Flash document (a *.fla* file) into a Flash movie (a *.swf* file) for testing in a debugging environment. To display text in the Test Movie mode's Output window, use the *trace()* function:

```
trace("Testing...testing...");
```

Text sent to the Output window appears in Test Movie mode only; to create a *.swf* file suitable for distribution (e.g., for display in a web browser), check the Omit Trace Actions option under File → Publish Settings → Flash, and click the Publish button in the Publish Settings dialog box. For details on embedding a *.swf* file in an HTML page, see "Working with Web Browsers." Use a dynamic text field to display text in the standalone or browser versions of the Flash Player.

Code Placement Best Practices

As a general rule, most code should reside on the main timeline of a project's main *.fla* file, on a frame labeled "main".

The "main" frame is not usually the first frame; instead, it typically follows any *preloader* code, which waits for the movie to load. Classes, long blocks of code, and large functions should be stored in external *.as* files (which are plain text files saved with the *.as* extension). Incorporate *.as* files into the document via the #include directive.

For example, a typical Flash application setup would be:

```
// PRELOADER ON FRAME 2 OF MAIN TIMELINE
if (this._framesloaded == this._totalframes) {
  this.gotoAndStop("main");
}

// CODE ON FRAME 3 OF MAIN TIMELINE
this.gotoAndPlay(2);

// CODE ON FRAME LABELED "main" OF THE MAIN TIMELINE
#include "SomeClass.as"
#include "SomeOtherClass.as"

init();

function init() {
  // ...start up application
}
```

For information on preloading code and content, see *http://design.oreilly.com/news/action_0501.html*. For more best practices, see *http://www.macromedia.com/desdev/mx/flash/whitepapers/actionscript_standards.pdf*.

Finding Code

If you're faced with a movie that seems to be missing important code, open the Actions panel and try these techniques for finding it:

- To search the current scene for ActionScript code, use the Movie Explorer search option (Window → Movie Explorer).
- With the Actions panel open, click on any frame in the timeline that contains a little "a" icon, which indicates

---

the presence of ActionScript code (the "a" may look like a tiny circle).

- Look for, and select, any white circle with a black outline on stage. Such circles indicate empty movie clips, which often contain code. If there's no code on the empty clip itself, double-click the clip to edit it, and investigate its frames.

- Select each button in the movie, one at a time. Some programmers place long, important scripts directly on buttons, instead of centralizing their code.

- Check the timeline for hidden or masked layers. A layer with a red X icon next to it is hidden during authoring, but may contain clips and buttons with code. Similarly, masked layers may also contain obscured objects that bear code. Unlock masked layers to reveal their contents.

- Unlock all layers. Empty movie clips (the little circles with black outlines) are hidden when the layer they're on is locked.

- In the Actions panel, use Ctrl+F (Windows) or Command+F (Macintosh) to open the Find dialog box. This is useful for searching large scripts for the specified text. (Use the Movie Explorer to search across all scripts.)

Using Movie Clips

Every Flash document contains a Stage, on which we place shapes, text, and other visual elements, and a main timeline, through which we define changes to the Stage's contents over time. The main timeline (i.e., the *main movie*) can contain independent submovies called *movie clips* (or *clips* for short). Each movie clip has its own independent timeline and *canvas* (the Stage is the canvas of the main movie) and can even contain other movie clips. A clip contained within another clip is called a *nested clip*. A clip that contains another clip is the nested clip's *parent clip*. The *playhead* represents the current slice in time (i.e., the active frame in a timeline). The duration of a frame is called a *tick*. For example, if the frame rate is 30 frames per second, a tick is 1/30 of a second.

A single Flash document can contain a hierarchy of inter-related movie clips. For example, the main movie may contain a mountainous landscape. A separate movie clip containing an animated character can be moved across the landscape to give the illusion that the character is walking. Each movie clip maintains a numbered *content stack* that governs how individual elements are layered visually at runtime (see "Movie Clip Depths").

ActionScript offers detailed control over movie clips. Each movie clip in a movie is an instance of the *MovieClip* class, so we can programmatically play a clip, stop it, move its playhead within its timeline, set its properties (such as its size, rotation, transparency level, and position on the Stage), and manipulate it as a true programming object. For a complete list of *MovieClip* properties and methods, consult the reference section in the latter half of this book.

Movie clips can be thought of as the raw material used to produce programmatically generated content in Flash. For example, a movie clip can serve as the ball or paddle in a pong game, as a drop-down list in an order form, or as a container for background sounds in an animation. Even Flash's built-in GUI components are created with movie clips.

Just as all object instances are based on a class, all movie clip instances are based on a template movie clip, called a *symbol*. Movie clip symbols live in the Library of each Flash document (*.fla* file).

To make a new, blank symbol, follow these steps:

1. Select Insert → New Symbol. The Create New Symbol dialog box appears.
2. In the Name field, type an identifier (i.e., a name) for the symbol.

---

3. For Behavior, select the Movie Clip radio button.

4. Click OK.

To make a new instance of a movie clip symbol at authoring time, click the symbol in the Library and drag it to the Stage. An instance created in this way should be named manually via the Property inspector. A movie clip's *instance name* is the identifier used to refer to it from ActionScript. Clips without instance names are given an automatic name that is not easily accessible via ActionScript. A clip's instance name should not be confused with the name of the symbol from which the clip was created, nor confused with the symbol's *linkage identifier*.

To set a symbol's linkage identifier (a.k.a. exporting the symbol), follow these steps:

1. In the Library, select the desired symbol.

2. In the Library's pop-up Options menu, select Linkage. The Linkage Properties dialog box appears.

3. Select the Export For ActionScript checkbox.

4. In the Identifier field, supply a unique name for the clip symbol. The name can be any string—often simply the same name as the symbol itself—but should be different from all other exported clip symbols.

To make a new instance of a movie clip symbol at runtime, use *MovieClip.attachMovie()*. For example, the following code creates a new instance of the symbol whose linkage identifier is boxSymbol and names the instance box_mc, placing it on depth 0 of the main timeline (see the next section, "Movie Clip Depths," for details on depths).

```
_root.attachMovie("boxSymbol", "box_mc", 0);
```

Be sure to set the symbol's linkage identifier (here, boxSymbol) before creating instances of it with *attachMovie()*.

To make a new generic movie clip instance (i.e., one with no symbol) at runtime, use *MovieClip.createEmptyMovieClip()*, which has the following syntax:

```
theClip.createEmptyMovieClip(newName, depth);
```

where *theClip* is a reference to the existing movie clip to which you want to attach a new, empty movie clip. The new clip instance is given a name of *newName* and placed in *theClip*'s content stack at the specified *depth*.

To delete a movie clip instance, use the *MovieClip.removeMovieClip()* method. For example, this code deletes box_mc:

```
box_mc.removeMovieClip();
```

Movie Clip Depths

Each movie clip instance, including the main timeline of a movie, places its various content (movie clips, text fields, and buttons) on one of two stacks: the internal layer stack (for author-time assets) or the programmatically generated content stack (for runtime assets). The items in these stacks (known collectively as the clip's *content stack*) are given an integer *depth* position that governs how they overlap on screen. Depth positions range from −16384 to 1048575. Depths from 0 to 1048575 are reserved for dynamically generated content; depths from −16383 to −1 are reserved for author-time content; and depth −16384 is reserved for dynamic content that appears beneath all author-time content in each clip (i.e., a runtime background). To retrieve the depth position of an item, use the *getDepth()* method. To switch the depth positions of two movie clips, use the *swapDepths()* method.

In addition to the content stack, Flash provides a *document stack* (or *level stack*) that governs the overlapping not of instances, but of entire *.swf* files loaded into the Player. The first *.swf* file loaded into the Flash Player is placed in the lowest level of the document stack (represented by the global property _level0). Using the *loadMovieNum()* global function, you can load additional *.swf* files into higher document levels, or even load a *.swf* file into _level0, replacing the base movie entirely. Once loaded, a movie can be referred to as _level*n*, where *n* is the level into which the movie was loaded.

Referring to Movie Clips

The main timeline of any Flash document is referred to by the global property _root. For example, the following code plays the document's main timeline:

```
_root.play();
```

From top-level statements on a movie clip's keyframe, the current clip can be referred to with the keyword this:

```
// Stops the current clip.
this.stop();
```

To access a nested clip, clipB, from a keyframe of its parent timeline, clipA, use a direct reference to clipB:

```
clipB._x = 30;   // Reposition clipB
```

To access the clip containing the current clip, use the _parent property:

```
// Make the parent clip 50% transparent
this._parent._alpha = 50;
```

ActionScript Syntax

ActionScript's syntax has much in common with JavaScript, Java, C, and C++. ActionScript uses curly braces to delimit statement blocks, parentheses for function invocation, and a dot for object property and method access. Here are the glamorous lexical rules of the language.

Comments

In ActionScript, single-line comments begin with // and end at the next carriage return:

```
// Some short code description goes here.
```

and multiline comments are delimited by /* and */:

```
/*
A longer description can go here. It can span multiple
lines without any problem.
*/
```

Whitespace

Whitespace characters (tabs, spaces, and carriage returns) are used in source code to separate programming tokens (keywords, identifiers, and expressions). Whitespace is optional when there is some other delimiter (such as an operator) that tells ActionScript where one token ends and another begins. Extra whitespace is ignored by the Action-Script interpreter. To break a statement onto more than one line, simply add a carriage return and keep typing, as the end of a statement is marked by a semicolon, not by a carriage return.

Statement Terminators (Semicolons)

The semicolon character (;) terminates an ActionScript statement. It is good practice to end your statements with semicolons, but semicolons are not strictly required. If the semicolon is omitted, the interpreter attempts to infer the end of a statement at each line break. Be sure not to use a semicolon after the #include directive or any pragmas.

Case Sensitivity

In ActionScript, keywords are case sensitive, but identifiers (such as variable names), frame labels, and symbol linkage identifiers are not. Even internal identifiers, such as property names and function names, are not case sensitive in Action-Script. Therefore, you can write gotoandplay() instead of gotoAndPlay(), or you can create a variable, password, and refer to it as passWORD. But you shouldn't do these things. If the case sensitivity rules ever change, your code may break.

Identifiers

ActionScript identifiers (variable and function names) must be composed according to the following rules:

- Must start with a letter, underscore, or dollar sign (not a number).
- Cannot be identical to reserved words.
- Should include only letters (A–Z or a–z), numbers, underscores, and dollar signs. Be especially careful never to use spaces, periods, backslashes, or other punctuation in identifiers.

Though not strictly required, it's also good practice to follow these rules when composing movie clip instance names, symbol names, symbol linkage identifiers, frame labels, and layer names.

Keywords

Table 1 lists keywords reserved for use by the ActionScript interpreter, and which therefore must not be used as identifiers.

Table 1. Current reserved keywords

add	else	in	onClipEvent	var
and	eq	instanceof	or	void
break	for	le	return	while
case	function	lt	super	with
continue	ge	ne	switch	
default	gt	new	tellTarget	
delete	if	not	this	
do	ifFrameLoaded	on	typeof	

Macromedia also reserves the keywords in Table 2 for potential future use, so avoid using them as identifiers as well.

Table 2. Potential future reserved keywords

abstract	debugger	float	native	synchronized
boolean	double	goto	package	throws
byte	enum	implements	private	transient
catch	export	import	protected	try
char	extends	int	public	volatile
class	final	interface	short	
const	finally	long	static	

Variables

ActionScript variables can contain any type of data and can be defined in one of three scopes: timeline, global, or local.

Timeline Variables

Timeline variables are variables declared with the *var* statement on a frame of a timeline, or in a button's *on()* handler or a movie clip's *onClipEvent()* handler. Once defined, timeline variables are accessible directly from any other frame on the same timeline, and indirectly via dot syntax from other movie clip timelines. For example:

```
// Declare timeline variable length
var length = 10;

// Assign a value to variable seenAlready
// in a nested movie clip, intro_mc
intro_mc.seenAlready = true;
```

To access timeline variables defined on the movie clip that contains the current movie clip, use _parent:

```
// Set velocity in the containing clip.
_parent.velocity = 10;

// Set language in the clip that contains
// the containing clip (two levels up
// the clip hierarchy).
_parent._parent.language = "English";
```

To access variables defined on a movie's main timeline, use _root or _level*n*, where *n* is a document level in the Flash Player. For example:

```
// Set x on the main timeline of the
// current movie.
_root.x = 10;

// Set y on the main timeline of the .swf
// file loaded into level 1.
_level1.y = 15;
```

Note, however, that if *movie1.swf* is loaded into a movie clip in *movie2.swf*, the _root property in *movie1.swf* refers to the main timeline of *movie2.swf*! To create an unchanging reference to a movie's main timeline, add the following code to frame 1 of the main timeline, substituting your movie's name for *movieName*:

```
_global.movieNameMainTimeline = this;
```

Thereafter, from any timeline in *movieName*, use *movieName*MainTimeline in place of _root.

Global Variables

Global variables are accessible from any timeline throughout any movie currently loaded into the Flash Player. To create a global variable, or to assign a global variable a new value, use:

```
_global.varName = value;
```

To read a global variable's value, simply refer to *varName* directly. For example:

```
// Create global variable numPlayers.
_global.numPlayers = 2;

// Pass numPlayers to startGame() function.
startGame(numPlayers);
```

When a timeline variable and a global variable have the same name, the timeline variable takes precedence (it *shadows* the global variable). To access a shadowed global variable, include _global before the variable name. For example:

```
_global.name = "Colin";   // Global variable
var name = "Bruce";        // Timeline variable
trace(name);               // Displays: Bruce
trace(_global.name);       // Displays: Colin
```

Local Variables

Local variables are created with the *var* statement in the body of a function. They are accessible within the function only, and they expire when the function finishes executing. For example, the following function uses two local variables, time and hour, in the calculation of the current hour:

```
// Returns the current hour, in
// 12-hour clock format.
function getHours12 () {
  var time = new Date();
  var hour = time.getHours();
  if (hour > 12) {
    hour -= 12;
  } else if (hour == 0) {
    hour = 12;
  }
  return hour;
}
```

Code Hinting

Table 3 lists the variable name suffixes that cause the Actions panel to display a quick-reference pop-up (so-called *code hinting*) when the variable name is entered. For example, to enable code hinting for a text field variable, you can name the variable output_txt.

Table 3. Code-hinting suffixes

Suffix	Datatype or class represented
_mc	MovieClip
_array	Array

Table 3. Code-hinting suffixes (continued)

Suffix	Datatype or class represented
_str	String
_btn	Button
_txt	TextField
_fmt	TextFormat
_date	Date
_sound	Sound
_xml	XML
_xmlsocket	XMLSocket
_color	Color
_video	Video
_ch	FCheckBox
_pb	FPushButton
_rb	FRadioButton
_lb	FListBox
_sb	FScrollBar
_cb	FComboBox
_sp	FScrollPane

Datatypes

ActionScript's built-in primitive datatypes are *number*, *string*, *boolean*, *undefined*, and *null*. ActionScript's built-in composite datatypes are *object*, *function*, and *movieclip*. ActionScript is a loosely typed language, which means that:

- Variables can hold any type of data
- Functions do not declare return types or parameter types
- Data containers (i.e., variables, array elements, and object properties) can change datatypes at any time
- Classes are not formally treated as distinct types (all classes are considered to be of type *object*)

When a value of one datatype is used in a context that requires a different datatype, the ActionScript interpreter automatically converts the value to the required datatype. For example, the *if* statement requires its test expression to be a Boolean value, but when a non-Boolean value is supplied as the test expression, ActionScript automatically converts it to a Boolean before the condition is checked. For example:

```
var options = new Array();
// The options array converts to the
// Boolean true, so the condition is met.
if (options) {
  displayOptions();
}
```

A value's type can also be changed manually, as explained later under "Explicit Datatype Conversion." The rules governing manual or automatic datatype conversions are listed in the following tables.

Datatype Conversion Rules

Table 4 shows the results of converting each datatype to a *number*.

Table 4. Converting to the number datatype

Original data	Result after conversion to number
undefined	0
null	0
Boolean	1 if the original value is true; 0 if the original value is false
Numeric string	Equivalent numeric value if string is composed only of base-10 numbers, whitespace, exponent, decimal point, plus sign, or minus sign (e.g., "-1.485e2")
Other strings	Empty strings and non-numeric strings, including strings starting with "x", "0x", or "FF", convert to NaN
"Infinity"	Infinity

Table 4. Converting to the number datatype (continued)

Original data	Result after conversion to number
"-Infinity"	-Infinity
"NaN"	NaN
Array	NaN
Object	The return value of the object's *valueOf( )* method
Movieclip	NaN

Table 5 shows the results of converting each datatype to a *string*.

Table 5. Converting to the string datatype

Original data	Result after conversion to string
undefined	"" (the empty string)
null	"null"
Boolean	"true" if the original value was true; "false" if the original value was false
NaN	"NaN"
0	"0"
Infinity	"Infinity"
-Infinity	"-Infinity"
Other numeric value	String equivalent of the number. For example, 944.345 becomes "944.345"
Array	A comma-separated list of element values
Object	The value that results from calling *toString( )* on the object; by default, the *toString( )* method of an object returns "[object Object]", but it can be customized (e.g., *toString( )* of a *Date* object returns a human-readable date such as: "Sun May 14 11:38:10 EDT 2000")
Movieclip	The path to the movie clip instance, given in absolute terms starting with the document level in the Player, e.g., "_level0.ball"

Table 6 shows the results of converting each datatype to a *boolean*.

Table 6. Converting to the boolean datatype

Original data	Result after conversion to boolean
undefined	false
null	false
NaN	false
0	false
Infinity	true
-Infinity	true
Other numeric value	true
Non-empty string	true if the string can be converted to a valid nonzero number, false if not; in ECMA-262, a non-empty string always converts to true (Flash diverges from the ECMA standard to maintain compatibility with Flash 4)
Empty string ("")	false
Array	true
Object	true
Movieclip	true

Explicit Datatype Conversion

Arbitrary values can be converted to the *string*, *number*, or *boolean* type as follows.

Converting to a string

A value can be converted to a string via the *toString()* method, the *String()* function, or by concatenating it with an empty string:

```
// Create a variable with a numeric value.
var i = 10;
// Convert i to a string with...
var a = i.toString();  // toString()
var b = String(i);     // String()
var c = i + "";        // Empty string concatenation
```

To convert a numeric value to a string representing the number in hexadecimal, use 16 as the radix argument of the *toString()* method:

```
var x = 255;
trace(x.toString(16));  // Displays: ff
```

Converting to a number

A value can be converted to a number via the *Number()*, *parseInt()*, and *parseFloat()* functions, or by subtracting 0:

```
// Create a variable with a Boolean value.
var flag = true;
// Convert flag to a number with...
var a = Number(flag);  // Number()
var b = flag - 0;      // Subtraction of 0
```

The *parseInt()* function extracts the first integer that appears in a string, provided that the string's first nonblank character is a legal numeric character. Otherwise, *parseInt()* yields NaN:

```
parseInt("1a")          // Yields 1
parseInt("1.3a")        // Yields 1
parseInt("Score: 2000") // Yields NaN
```

To convert a hexadecimal string to a decimal number, either prefix the hexadecimal string with "0x":

```
// Parsed as hex, (implicit radix of 16) yields 255
parseInt("0xFF")
```

or specify 16 as the radix (*parseInt()*'s second argument):

```
// Parsed as hex, (explicit radix of 16) yields 255
parseInt("FF", 16)
```

The *parseFloat()* function returns the first floating-point number that appears in a string, provided that the string's first nonblank character is a valid numeric character. Otherwise, *parseFloat()* yields NaN:

```
// Yields 2.5
parseFloat("2.5 is your total")
// Yields NaN
parseFloat("Total: 2.5")
```

Converting to a Boolean

A value can be converted to a Boolean with the *Boolean()* function:

```
var obj = new Object();
// Yields true (in accordance with Table 6)
Boolean(obj)
```

Determining Datatype and Class

To check the datatype of any value, use the *typeof* operator:

```
trace(typeof 11);    // Displays: "number"
var name = "Gary";
trace(typeof name);  // Displays: "string"
```

To check whether an object belongs to a particular class, use the *instanceof* operator. The following code creates a new *Array* instance and checks whether that instance belongs to the *Array* class:

```
var list = ["one", "two", "three"];
// Displays: true
trace(list instanceof Array);
```

The number Datatype

ActionScript provides a single datatype, *number*, to represent all integer and floating-point numeric values (in double-precision, floating-point format, which offers precision to about 15 significant digits). A numeric literal consists of a sequence of digits, followed by an optional decimal point, followed by an optional exponent:

```
3
3.14
15e5   // The number 1500000
```

A leading sign (+ or -) is optional. A leading 0x indicates hexadecimal (base-16), while a leading 0 (zero) indicates octal (base-8):

```
0xCC  // The decimal number 204 is "CC" in hexadecimal
```

Table 7 lists the special values of the *number* datatype.

Table 7. Special values of the number datatype

Value	Description
NaN	Value returned by numeric error condition, such as dividing zero by itself or datatype conversion failure
Number.MIN_VALUE	Smallest representable numeric value (smaller values, considered an underflow, result in 0)
Number.MAX_VALUE	Largest representable numeric value (larger values, considered an overflow, result in Infinity)
Infinity	Any number larger than Number.MAX_VALUE (i.e., the result of a positive overflow)
-Infinity	Any number more negative than -Number.MAX_VALUE (i.e., the result of a negative overflow)

The string Datatype

The *string* datatype is used for textual data (letters, punctuation marks, and other characters). A string literal is any combination of characters enclosed in single or double quotation marks. For example:

```
"Welcome to my website."  // Double quotes
'Welcome to my website.'  // Single quotes
```

A string delimited by double quotation marks must use a backslash to *escape* any double quotation marks within the string itself, as follows:

```
"She said, \"Hi\" to me"
```

As of Flash Player 6, a Unicode escape sequence can be used to include any Unicode character via its numeric code point. A Unicode escape sequence starts with a backslash and a lowercase *u* (i.e., \u) followed by the four-digit hex number of the character's code point. For example:

```
\u00A9  // The copyright symbol
\u2014  // The em dash
```

In Flash Player 5, all Unicode (\u) escape sequences must reference a code point in the Latin 1 or Shift-JIS character sets; other Unicode characters will not display correctly.

To ease the entry of common special characters, Action-Script also provides several shorthand escape sequences, listed in Table 8.

Table 8. Escape sequences

Escape sequence	Meaning
\b	Backspace character (ASCII 8)
\f	Form feed character (ASCII 12)
\n	Newline character; causes a line break (ASCII 10)
\r	Carriage return (CR) character; causes a line break (ASCII 13)
\t	Tab character (ASCII 9)
\'	Single quotation mark
\"	Double quotation mark
\\	Backslash character; necessary when using backslash as a literal character, to prevent \ from being interpreted as the beginning of an escape sequence
\x*dd*	Character with Latin-1 encoding specified by two hexadecimal digits *dd*
\u*dddd*	Character with Unicode encoding specified by four hexadecimal digits *dddd*

Unicode characters can also be created by passing a comma-delimited list of decimal or hexadecimal character code points to *String.fromCharCode()*, which returns the corresponding characters. For example, the following expression yields a copyright symbol:

```
String.fromCharCode(169)
```

Although Flash Player 6 fully supports Unicode, the Flash MX authoring tool does not. The Flash MX authoring tool allows entry of characters from the Latin 1, Shift-JIS, and

MacRoman character sets only. To include characters from other languages, you must do one of the following:

- At runtime, use *XML.load()* or *LoadVars.load()* to import an external Unicode-formatted XML or variables file

- At authoring time, save text in an external Unicode-formatted text file with the *.as* extension, then import that file using the #include directive

- At authoring time, create each character individually using either the standard Unicode hex escape sequence or *String.fromCharCode()*

For example, the following code creates a global variable, euro, that contains the euro sign character. The euro variable is used by the price_txt text field for display on screen.

```
_global.euro = "\u20AC";
this.createTextField("price_txt", 1, 100, 100, 200, 20);
price_txt.text = "99 " + euro;
```

When a primitive string value is used in a context that expects a *String* object, ActionScript automatically "wraps" the value in a *String* object for the sake of the operation. This allows us to invoke methods such as *charAt()* or *indexOf()* on a string, for example, or to check the number of characters in a string with the length property.

```
var name = "Colin";
trace(name.indexOf("b"));   // Displays: -1
trace(name.length);         // Displays: 5
```

For a complete list of methods and properties that you can use with strings, see the *String* class in the reference section.

The boolean Datatype

Boolean data is used to represent the logical states of truth and falsehood. Hence there are only two legal values of the *boolean* datatype: true and false (without quotation marks). Boolean values are most commonly used in loops and conditional statements.

The null and undefined Datatypes

To represent the absence of data, ActionScript provides the *null* and *undefined* datatypes, whose single legal values are, respectively, null and undefined.

The undefined value is returned by the interpreter automatically whenever a variable, property, or array element is accessed but does not exist or has not yet been assigned a value.

By contrast, the null value is used by programmers to indicate that a variable, property, or array element intentionally has no value.

Note that null and undefined are considered equal by the == operator. To test explicitly for one but not the other, use the strict equality operator, ===, which consists of three equals signs. The strict equality operator tests first whether two expressions are of the same datatype before testing whether they have the same value.

The object Datatype

ActionScript uses the *object* datatype to hold collections of logically related data values (called *properties*) and functions (called *methods*). See "Object-Oriented ActionScript" for details.

The function Datatype

The *function* datatype represents ActionScript functions, which are reusable code fragments (also known as *subroutines* in some languages). For information on using functions, see "Creating and Using Functions."

The movieclip Datatype

The *movieclip* datatype represents movie clips, the basic content containers of Flash. Movie clips are used exactly like objects, but belong to their own datatype due to the way they are allocated and deallocated by the interpreter (see *http://moock.org/asdg/technotes/movieclipDatatype/*). For information on movie clips, see "Using Movie Clips."

Arrays

Arrays are used to manage a collection of data values in a simple list (ActionScript does not supply any higher-level data structures for collection management). An ActionScript array has the following characteristics:

- It can be resized dynamically at runtime
- It can contain values of any datatype (even mixed datatypes within a single array)
- It uses a zero-relative index to refer to its *elements* (the values it contains)

To create a new array, use the *Array* constructor:

```
var list = new Array(value1, value2);
```

or use an array literal, delimited with square brackets:

```
var list = [value1, value2];
```

To add a new element to an array, assign a value using the element's index number within square brackets:

```
list[2] = value3;
list[3] = value4;
```

To remove an element, use *splice()* (to delete it from the middle of an array), or *shift()* and *pop()* (to delete it from the beginning or end of an array):

```
// list becomes [value1, value3, value4]
list.splice(1, 1);
// list becomes [value3, value4]
list.shift();
// list becomes [value3]
list.pop();
```

Other array methods, such as *push()*, *unshift()*, and *sort()*, are listed in the reference section.

To enumerate all the numbered elements of an array, use a *for* loop:

```
var games = ["Quake", "Ico", "Zelda"];
for (var i = 0; i < games.length; i++) {
  trace("Game " + i + " is " + games[i]);
}
```

The following code does the same thing but more than twice as fast, because it calculates the length of the array only once. (However, this version counts down through the array.)

```
var games = ["Quake", "Ico", "Zelda"];
for (var i = games.length; --i >= 0;) {
  trace("Game " + i + " is " + games[i]);
}
```

To create an *associative array*, which allows you to access elements by name rather than by number, simply add named properties to an *Array* instance (exactly as properties are added to any object):

```
var userAccount = new Array();
userAccount.totalCash = 950;
```

Arrays can be nested (i.e., they can be multidimensional):

```
var titeRow = ["Name", "Description"];
var row1 = ["Mario", "Classic game"];
var row2 = ["Sly Cooper", "Great game"];
var games = [titleRow, row1, row2];
```

To access nested elements, use the array access operator ([ ]) in succession:

```
// Access the description of Sly Cooper:
var slyDesc = games[2][1];
```

Operators

Table 9 lists the precedence ("P") and the associativity ("A") for ActionScript operators. Precedence determines which operations within an expression are performed first. Associativity determines whether the operation is performed left to right ("L") or right to left ("R").

Table 9. Operator precedence and associativity

P	A	Operator	Description
15	L	.	Object property access
15	L	[]	Array element access
15	L	()	Parentheses
15	L	function()	Function call
14	L	x++	Postfix increment
14	L	x--	Postfix decrement
14	R	++x	Prefix increment
14	R	--x	Prefix decrement
14	R	-	Unary negation
14	R	~	Bitwise *NOT*
14	R	!	Logical *NOT*
14	R	new	Create object/array
14	R	delete	Remove object/property/array element
14	R	typeof	Determine datatype
14	R	void	Return undefined value
13	L	*	Multiply
13	L	/	Divide
13	L	%	Modulo division
12	L	+	Addition or string concatenation
12	L	-	Subtraction
11	L	<<	Bitwise left shift
11	L	>>	Bitwise signed right shift
11	L	>>>	Bitwise unsigned right shift
10	L	<	Less than
10	L	<=	Less than or equal to

Table 9. Operator precedence and associativity (continued)

P	A	Operator	Description
10	L	>	Greater than
10	L	>=	Greater than or equal to
10	L	instanceof	Check an object's class
9	L	==	Equality
9	L	!=	Not equal to
9	L	===	Strict equality
9	L	!==	Strict inequality
8	L	&	Bitwise *AND*
7	L	^	Bitwise *XOR*
6	L	|	Bitwise *OR*
5	L	&&	Logical *AND*
4	L	||	Logical *OR*
3	R	?:	Conditional
2	R	=	Assignment
2	R	+=	Add and reassign
2	R	−=	Subtract and reassign
2	R	*=	Multiply and reassign
2	R	/=	Divide and reassign
2	R	%=	Modulo division and reassign
2	R	<<=	Bit-shift left and reassign
2	R	>>=	Bit-shift right and reassign
2	R	>>>=	Bit-shift right (unsigned) and reassign
2	R	&=	Bitwise *AND* and reassign
2	R	^=	Bitwise *XOR* and reassign
2	R	|=	Bitwise *OR* and reassign
1	L	,	Comma

Conditionals and Loops

ActionScript's control statements (*conditionals* and *loops*) borrow syntax directly from Java and C++. They include *if–else if–else*, *switch*, *while*, *do-while*, *for*, and *for-in*.

The if–else if–else Statements

An *if* statement creates a two-pronged code branch, like a fork in the road. It has the following syntax:

```
if (condition) {
   substatements
}
```

Note the use of curly braces ({}) to delimit the code block containing one or more statements.

If *condition* resolves to the Boolean value true, then the *substatements* are executed. For example:

```
var x = 10;
if (x == 10) {
   // This code executes only if x is 10.
   trace("The value of x is 10");
}
```

Using an *else* statement, we can specify an alternative statement block to execute when an *if* condition is false:

```
if (condition) {
   substatements1
} else {
   substatements2
}
```

In that case, *substatements1* will be executed if *condition* is true; *substatements2* will be executed if *condition* is false.

By using *if* and *else if*, we can optionally execute one (or even none) of an unlimited number of code blocks. Like *else*, *else if* is a syntactic extension of an *if* statement:

```
if (condition1) {
   substatements1
```

```
} else if (condition2) {
  substatements2
} else if (condition3) {
  substatements3
} else {
  // Catchall if other conditions were not met
  substatements4
}
```

Here, *substatements1* will be executed if *condition1* is true. If *condition1* is false and *condition2* is true, *substatements2* will be executed. Otherwise, *condition3* is evaluated, and the process continues for as many *else if* statements as are provided. If none of the test expressions are true, *substatements4* in the final catchall *else* clause will be executed.

The switch Statement

The *switch* statement, introduced in Flash Player 6, executes one (or sometimes more) of several possible code blocks, based on the value of a single test expression.

The general form of the *switch* statement is:

```
switch (testExpression) {
  case expression1:
    substatements1
    break;
  case expression2:
    substatements2
    break;
  default:
    substatements3
    break;
}
```

where *testExpression* is a value that the interpreter will attempt to match with each of the supplied *case expressions*, from top to bottom. The case expressions are supplied after the keyword case and are followed by a colon. If *testExpression* matches a case expression, all statements immediately following that case expression are executed, including those in any subsequent case blocks! To prevent subsequent blocks from executing, we must use the *break* statement at the end of each block. If no case expression matches *testExpression*, all statements following the *default* label are executed.

For example, in the following *switch* statement, we greet the user with a custom message depending on the value of the test expression gender:

```
var surname = "Porter";
var gender = "male";
switch (gender) {
  case "femaleMarried":
    trace("Hello Mrs. " + surname);
    break;
  case "femaleGeneric":
    trace("Hello Ms. " + surname);
    break;
  case "male":
    trace("Hello Mr. " + surname);
    break;
  default:
    trace("Hello " + surname);
}
```

The while Statement

The *while* statement executes a section of code repeatedly. It has the following syntax:

```
while (condition) {
  substatements
}
```

For as long as *condition* is true, *substatements* are executed repeatedly. Typically, *substatements* contain some code that eventually causes *condition* to become false. Here's an example loop that counts to 10:

```
var i = 1;
while (i <= 10) {
  trace("i is " + i);
  i++;
}
```

The do-while Statement

A *do-while* statement always executes at least once before looping (repeating). It has the following syntax:

```
do {
  substatements
} while (condition);
```

On the interpreter's first pass through the *do-while* loop, *substatements* are executed before *condition* is ever checked. At the end of the *substatements* block, if *condition* is true, the loop begins anew and *substatements* are executed again. The loop executes repeatedly until *condition* becomes false.

The for Statement

A *for* loop is essentially synonymous with a *while* loop, but it is written with more compact syntax:

```
for (initialization; condition; update) {
  substatements
}
```

Before the first iteration of a *for* loop, the *initialization* statement runs, typically creating an *iterator variable*, such as i, or count. Then, if *condition* is true, *substatements* are executed. Finally, the *update* statement is executed. If, after *update* completes, *condition* is still true, *substatements* are executed again (and the process repeats until *condition* becomes false).

Here's a typical *for* loop that simply counts from 1 to 10. Compare it with the equivalent *while* loop shown earlier.

```
for (var i = 1; i <= 10; i++) {
  trace("i is " + i);
}
```

The for-in Statement

A *for-in* statement is a specialized loop used to enumerate the properties of an object. It has the following syntax:

```
for (var thisProp in someObject) {
  // Substatements typically use thisProp in some way
  substatements
}
```

The *substatements* are executed once for each property of *someObject*, which is a reference to any valid object. During each loop iteration, the *thisProp* variable is automatically set to a string that is the name of the object property currently being enumerated. For example, the following code creates an object and enumerates its properties with a *for-in* loop:

```
var ball = new Object();
ball.radius = 12;
ball.color = "red";
ball.style = "beach";
for (var prop in ball) {
  trace("ball has the property " + prop);
}
```

Because prop reflects the names of the properties of ball as strings, we can use the [] operator with prop to retrieve the values of those properties, like this:

```
for (var prop in ball) {
  trace("Found property: " + prop
        + ", with value: " + ball[prop]);
}
```

The following example uses a *for-in* loop to detect and play all the movie clips on the main timeline (_root):

```
// Check all the properties of the main timeline.
for (prop in _root) {
  // If this property is a movie clip...
  if (typeof _root[prop] == "movieclip") {
    // ...play the clip
    _root[prop].play();
  }
}
```

The break and continue Statements

The *break* statement ends the execution of the current loop or *switch* statement. For example, the following example uses a loop to search through a string for the letter "z". If "z" is found, the loop is terminated by the *break* statement.

```
var phrase = "Candians pronounce z, 'zed'";
for (var i = 0; i < phrase.length; i++) {
  if (phrase.charAt(i) == "z") {
    trace("z found at index " + i);
    break;
  }
}
```

The *continue* statement is similar to the *break* statement in that it causes the current iteration of a loop to be aborted, but unlike *break*, it resumes the loop's execution with the next natural cycle.

Loops, Screen Updates, and Maximum Iterations

In ActionScript, it is impossible to update the screen from within the body of a *while*, *do-while*, *for*, or *for-in* statement. Furthermore, loops execute for a maximum of 15 seconds before the Flash Player displays a warning dialog box. To overcome these limitations, we can use a timeline loop, a *MovieClip.onEnterFrame()* event handler, or the *setInterval()* function.

To make an infinite timeline loop that allows the screen to refresh between iterations, follow these steps:

1. Create a new Flash movie.
2. On frame 1, attach the body of the loop:

   ```
   // Repeated code goes here.
   trace("Hi there! Welcome to frame 1");
   ```

3. On frame 2, add a blank keyframe and attach the following statement:

   ```
   this.gotoAndPlay(1);
   ```

The preceding timeline loop monopolizes the timeline it's on. To execute code once per tick of the frame rate without looping the timeline, use a *MovieClip.onEnterFrame()* event handler, as follows:

1. Create a new Flash movie.

2. On frame 1, attach the following code:

```
// We use _root here, but it could be any movie clip.
_root.onEnterFrame = function () {
  // Repeated code goes here.
  trace("This statement repeats.");
}
```

For more information on event handlers, particularly regarding the scope of statements in an event handler, see the upcoming section "Event Handling."

The frequency of code execution in a timeline loop or a *MovieClip.onEnterFrame()* event handler is governed by the movie's frame rate. To execute a function every *n* milliseconds (independent of the movie's frame rate), use *setInterval()*. For example, the following code executes the *doSomething()* function every 20 milliseconds:

```
function doSomething () {
  // Repeated code goes here.
  trace("This code repeats");
  // To refresh the screen, include the following line:
  updateAfterEvent();
}
intervalID = setInterval(doSomething, 20);
```

To stop the repetition, use:

```
clearInterval(intervalID);
```

Creating and Using Functions

ActionScript functions are procedural-style subroutines that are created once but can be executed whenever needed throughout a movie. Functions are normally created on a keyframe in a timeline, but they can also be defined inside a movie clip's *onClipEvent()* handler or a button's *on()* handler. They can even be nested within other functions.

The following syntax declares a new function:

```
function funcName (param1,...paramn) {
  statements
}
```

where *funcName* is the function's legal identifier, *param1, ... paramn* are the function parameters, and *statements* is the code executed when the function is invoked. Functions can also be declared as literal values and stored in variables, object properties, or array elements. For example:

```
// Store a function literal in the
// variable getRandomInt.
var getRandomInt = function (min, max) {
  return minVal + Math.floor(Math.random()
        * (maxVal + 1 - minVal));
}
```

To invoke a function without passing it any arguments, supply the function name followed by the function call operator, ():

```
funcName()
```

To pass arguments to a function, provide a comma-separated list of values within parentheses when invoking the function:

```
funcName(arg1, arg2,...argn)
```

To return a data value from a function, use the *return* statement (i.e., the return keyword followed by the expression to be returned). For example, this function returns the value true if its parameter is an even number, and false otherwise:

```
function isEven (n) {
  return n%2 == 0;
}
```

When no return expression is specified, the *return* statement simply terminates a function (and returns the value undefined). For example, this function exits promptly when passed a value for guess that does not match the correct password. (Here, password would either be a global variable, or it would be defined in the same movie clip as the *enterSite()* function.)

```
function enterSite(guess) {
  if (guess != password) {
    // Wrong password, so quit.
    return;
  }
  // Proceed with site-entry code.
}
```

Like a variable, a function created in a movie clip can be accessed as a property of that clip. For example, function *submit()* in movie clip form_mc can be invoked as form_mc.submit(). Or function *randomize()* on the main timeline can be invoked as _root.randomize() from anywhere in the movie.

Within a function, temporary local variables can be created with the *var* statement. For example:

```
function randomRotate (theClip) {
  // angle is a local variable that expires
  // when the function exits.
  var angle = Math.floor(Math.random() * 360) - 180;
  theClip._rotation = angle;
}
```

When retrieving a variable's value within a function, the interpreter first looks for the variable in the local scope, then in any parent functions (if the function is nested), then in the movie clip where the function was declared, and finally in the global scope.

For example, the following function uses *setInterval()* to execute a nested function after a delay. The nested function, *callFunc()*, can refer directly to its parent function's local variable, id, in the expression clearInterval(id).

```
// Use a function literal to assign the
// function to a global variable, setTimeout
```

```
_global.setTimeout = function (func, delay) {
  var id = setInterval(callFunc, delay);
  // Define nested funtion, callFunc()
  function callFunc () {
    clearInterval(id);
    func();
  }
}

// Usage:
setTimeout(sayHi, 1000);

function sayHi () {
  trace("hello world");
}
```

In ActionScript, functions are instances of the *Function* class and can be stored and passed as data, like any other object. Furthermore, as objects, functions can have properties. For sample uses of functions as objects, see the sections "Event Handling" and "Object-Oriented ActionScript," and the *Function* class in the reference section.

Event Handling

ActionScript provides four distinct mechanisms for handling events: event handler properties, listener events, *onClipEvent()* handlers, and *on()* handlers.

Event Handler Properties

Event handler properties are predefined methods invoked automatically by a class. (They are referred to as "properties" because in ActionScript, a method is a property that stores a function object.) The general form of an event handler property is:

```
someObject.someEventHandler = function () {
  statements
};
```

where *someObject* is an object that generates events, *someEventHandler* is the name of the event, and `statements` is the code to execute when the event occurs. For example, the following *MovieClip.onEnterFrame()* handler rotates the main timeline by five degrees for every tick of the frame rate:

```
_root.onEnterFrame = function () {
  this._rotation += 5;
}
```

Notice that within the handler, the object that fired the event is referred to by the keyword this.

The following *Button* class *onPress()* handler submits a form when submit_btn is pressed:

```
submit_btn.onPress = function () {
  // submitForm() is a custom function
  // defined in the movie clip in which
  // this button resides (this._parent)
  this._parent.submitForm();
}
```

In Flash MX, the following core classes define event handler properties:

Button	Sound
LoadVars	TextField
LocalConnection	XML
MovieClip	XMLSocket
SharedObject	

Event Listeners

Some classes and objects broadcast event notices to all subscribed *listeners* (objects that have registered to be notified when a given event occurs). In general terms, an event listener object responds to an event as follows:

```
listenerObject.eventName = function () {
  statements
}
eventSource.addListener(listenerObject);
```

where *listenerObject* is the object registering to be notified of the event, *eventName* is the name of the event, and *eventSource* is the object that broadcasts the event. For example, the following code creates a listener object that prints a message to the Output window when the mouse button is pressed over the movie:

```
// Create a generic object (although
// a listener can be any type of object)
mouseListener = new Object();

// Assign a callback function
// to the object's onMouseDown property
mouseListener.onMouseDown = function () {
  trace("The mouse was pressed!");
}

// Register the listener with the Mouse object
Mouse.addListener(mouseListener);
```

In Flash MX, the following core classes define listener events: *Key*, *Mouse*, *Selection*, *Stage*, and *TextField*.

The onClipEvent( ) and on( ) Event Handlers

As we've seen, the *Button* and *MovieClip* classes define event handler properties. These two classes also support a special event handler syntax for code attached directly to physical movie clips or buttons in the Flash authoring tool.

Button instances can define *on()* handlers of the form:

```
on (eventName) {
  statements
}
```

where *eventName* is the name of the corresponding *Button* class event handler property, without the word "on" and with the first letter lowercased. For example, the equivalent *on()* handler version of the *onRelease()* event handler property would be:

```
on (release) {
  statements
}

// Same as:
someButton.onRelease = function () {
  statements
}
```

Movie clip instances can also define button *on()* handlers (as of Flash MX) and additionally support *onClipEvent()* handlers of the form:

```
onClipEvent (eventName) {
  statements
}
```

Again, the *eventName* is the name of the corresponding *MovieClip* class event handler property, with the word "on" removed.

To create a sample button *on()* handler, follow these instructions:

1. Create a new, blank Flash movie.

2. Create a button and drag an instance of it onto the main Stage.

3. With the button selected, enter the following code in the Actions panel:

   ```
   on (release) {
     trace("You clicked the button");
   }
   ```

4. Select Control → Test Movie.

5. Click the button you created. The message "You clicked the button" appears in the Output window.

To create a sample movie clip *onClipEvent()* handler, follow these instructions:

1. Create a new, blank Flash movie.

2. On the main movie Stage, draw a rectangle.

3. Select Insert → Convert to Symbol.

4. In the Convert to Symbol dialog box, name the new symbol **rectangle**, and select Movie Clip as the Behavior.

5. Click OK to finish creating the *rectangle* movie clip.

6. Select the *rectangle* clip on stage, and then enter the following in the Actions panel:

```
onClipEvent (keyDown) {
  this._visible = false;
}
onClipEvent (keyUp) {
  this._visible = true;
}
```

7. Select Control → Test Movie.

Click the movie to make sure it has keyboard focus, then press and hold any key. Each time you depress a key, the *rectangle* movie clip disappears. Each time you release the depressed key, *rectangle* reappears.

NOTE

Generally, event handler properties and event listeners are preferred over *onClipEvent()* and *on()* handlers because they promote the separation of code from the visual elements of a movie.

The following summarizes the scope of statements in the various types of event handlers. For handlers and listeners assigned within a function (denoted with an asterisk), the scope is that function (in accordance with the rules of nested function scope, discussed earlier).

*Event handler property**
  Example:

```
someTextField.onSetFocus = function () {
  statements
}
```

The scope is the clip in which function declaration occurred.

---

*Event listener method**

Example:

```
GUIManager.onResize = function () {
  statements
}
Stage.addListener(GUIManager);
```

The scope is the clip in which function declaration occurred.

*MovieClip with event handler property**

Example:

```
theClip_mc.onPress = function () {
  statements
}
```

The scope is the clip in which function declaration occurred.

MovieClip with on() handler

Example:

```
on (press) {
  statements
}
```

The scope is the clip that bears the handler in the authoring tool.

MovieClip with onClipEvent() handler

Example:

```
onClipEvent (enterFrame) {
  statements
}
```

The scope is the clip that bears the handler in the authoring tool.

*Button with event handler property**

Example:

```
submit_btn.onRelease = function () {
  statements
}
```

The scope is the clip in which function declaration occurred.

Button with on() handler

Example:

```
on (release) {
  statements
}
```

The scope is the clip on whose timeline the button resides.

Table 10 summarizes the values of the this keyword in the various types of event handlers.

Table 10. Value of the this keyword within event handlers

Event handling mechanism	Value of the this keyword
Event handler property	The object that defines the handler property.
Event listener method	The object registered as a listener.
MovieClip with event handler property	The movie clip that defines the handler property.
MovieClip with *on()* handler	The movie clip that bears the handler in the authoring tool.
MovieClip with *onClipEvent()* handler	The movie clip that bears the handler in the authoring tool.
Button with event handler property	The button that defines the handler property.
Button with *on()* handler	The movie clip on whose timeline the button resides.

Object-Oriented ActionScript

ActionScript does not enforce object orientation. Indeed, many projects can be created with a well thought out set of variables and procedural-style functions. However, Action-Script does offer object-oriented programming facilities. In fact, most of ActionScript's built-in capabilities are exposed through classes and objects (listed in the reference section of this book).

To create a class, simply define a constructor function:

```
function ClassName (param1, param2) {
  // ...constructor code goes here...
}
```

To create instance properties for a class, assign values to property names inside the class constructor function:

```
function ClassName (param1, param2) {
  // Instance properties
  this.propName1 = param1;
  this.propName2 = param2;
}
```

After creating properties, initialize the object:

```
function ClassName (param1, param2) {
  // Instance properties
  this.propName1 = param1;
  this.propName2 = param2;

  // Initialize object.
  // ...initialization code goes here...
}
```

To create an instance method, assign a function to a property of the class constructor's built-in prototype property:

```
ClassName.prototype.methodName = function () {
  // ...method body goes here...
};
```

To refer to an instance within a method, use the this keyword:

```
ClassName.prototype.methodName = function () {
  this.propName1 = value;
  this.doSomething();
};
```

To create a property that is static (also called a "class property"), define it on the class constructor function:

```
ClassName.staticPropName = value;
```

To create a method that is static (also called a "class method"), define it on the class constructor function:

```
ClassName.staticMethodName = function () {
  // ...method body goes here...
};
```

To create a subclass, set the prototype property of the class constructor function to an instance of the superclass:

```
function SubClass (param1, param2) {
  // ...constructor code goes here...
}
// DO THIS BEFORE
// DEFINING SubClass's METHODS!
SubClass.prototype = new SuperClass();
```

To create a new instance of a class, use the *new* operator:

```
var someInstance = new ClassName();
```

To invoke a method on an instance, use the dot operator and the function call operator:

```
someInstance.someMethod();
```

Alternatively, use the [ ] operator, specifying the name of the method as any string expression:

```
someInstance["someMethod"]();
```

To set or retrieve the value of a property, use the dot operator:

```
// Set
someInstance.propName = value;
// Retrieve
var someVar = someInstance.propName;
```

Alternatively, use the [ ] operator, specifying the name of the property as any string expression:

```
// Set
someInstance["propName"] = value;
// Retrieve
var someVar = someInstance["propName"];
```

Working with Graphics

Graphical content in Flash is typically created in the authoring tool itself, using the application's various drawing tools. Primitive shapes drawn at authoring time, however, are not directly scriptable. To create graphical content at authoring time that can be moved, rotated, and otherwise manipulated at runtime, place that content in a movie clip instance and control that instance via the *MovieClip* class's methods and properties.

Primitive lines and fills can also be created in a movie clip at runtime with the Drawing API, which includes the following drawing methods:

```
MovieClip.beginFill( )
MovieClip.beginGradientFill( )
MovieClip.clear( )
MovieClip.curveTo( )
MovieClip.endFill( )
MovieClip.lineStyle( )
MovieClip.lineTo( )
MovieClip.moveTo( )
```

For example, the following code draws a square in the current movie clip:

```
// Set stroke to 3-point
this.lineStyle(3);
// Move the pen to 100 pixels left and
// above the registration point
this.moveTo(-100,-100);
// Start our red square shape
this.beginFill(0xFF0000);
// Draw the lines of our square
this.lineTo(100, -100);
this.lineTo(100, 100);
this.lineTo(-100, 100);
this.lineTo(-100, -100);
// Close our red square shape
this.endFill();
```

For a variety of interesting applications of the Drawing API (including drawing arcs, polygons, dashed lines, stars, and wedges), see the following articles:

- *http://www.formequalsfunction.com/downloads/ drawmethods.html*
- *http://www.macromedia.com/desdev/mx/flash/articles/ precision_drawing.html*

Working with Text

Text on screen in a Flash movie is accessible to ActionScript via the *TextField* class. Each *TextField* object represents a rectangular text container that can be formatted, sized, or filled with text, and can receive user input.

TextField objects are not constructed with the *new* operator; instead, they are created automatically by Flash whenever author-time text is drawn (with the Text tool) or when the *MovieClip.createTextField()* method is invoked. For example, the following code creates a text field in the current movie clip, names it output_txt, and places it on depth 1, at Stage coordinates (0,0), with a width of 200 and a height of 20.

```
this.createTextField("output_txt", 1, 0, 0, 200, 20);
```

Text fields created at authoring time are accessible to Action-Script only when their type is set to Dynamic Text or Input Text and they have been assigned an instance name via the Property inspector. To create an ActionScript-controllable text field at authoring time, perform the following steps:

1. Select the Text tool.
2. Drag a rectangle big enough to display the desired text on stage.
3. Make sure the Property inspector (Window → Properties) is open.

4. In the Property inspector, for Type, select Dynamic Text or Input Text (Static Text cannot be accessed through ActionScript).

5. In the Property inspector, for Instance Name, supply a legal identifier for the text field. An Instance Name cannot be specified until Type is set, as described in Step 4.

To assign text for display in a text field, use the text property:

```
output_txt.text = "Hello world";
```

To add a border around a text field, set the border property to true:

```
output_txt.border = true;
```

To add a background to a text field, set the background property to true:

```
output_txt.background = true;
```

To change the border color, set the borderColor property using hexadecimal RGB triplet notation:

```
output_txt.borderColor = 0xFF0000; // Red
```

To change the background color, set the backgroundColor property:

```
output_txt.backgroundColor = 0xCCCCCC;
```

To force the border to automatically resize to fit a text field's content, set the autoSize property to true:

```
output_txt.autoSize = true;
```

To display rudimentary HTML in a text field, set the html property to true and assign HTML source to the htmlText property:

```
output_txt.html = true;
output_txt.htmlText = "wow, <B>bold!</B>";
```

The set of HTML tags supported by Flash 5 text fields includes <B>, <I>, <U>, <FONT> (with FACE, SIZE, and COLOR attributes), <P>, <BR>, and <A>. Flash 6 adds support for <LI>

and <TEXTFORMAT> (with LEFTMARGIN, RIGHTMARGIN, BLOCK-INDENT, INDENT, LEADING, and TABSTOPS attributes corresponding to the *TextFormat* class's properties of the same names).

To prevent the user from selecting the text in a text field, set the selectable property to false:

```
output_txt.selectable = false;
```

To easily change the color of all text in a text field, set the textColor property:

```
output_txt.textColor = 0xFF0000;   // red
```

To allow the user to enter new text in a text field, set the type property to "input" and the selectable property to true:

```
output_txt.type = "input";
output_txt.selectable = true;
```

To position a text field, use the _x and _y properties:

```
output_txt._x = 300;
output_txt._y = 200;
```

To scroll text to a given line, set the scroll property to the desired line number (the first line's index is 1):

```
// Create three lines.
output_txt.text = "hello\nthere\nworld";
// Scroll to line 2.
output_txt.scroll = 2;
```

To delete a text field, use the *removeTextField()* method:

```
output_txt.removeTextField();
```

For more text fun, see the *TextField* class in the reference section. For advanced text formatting tools, see the *TextFormat* class.

GUIs and Components

Flash MX introduces so-called *components*—reusable, packaged code modules that add a particular capability to a Flash movie. Components can include graphics as well as code, so they're neat little bundles of self-contained functionality that you can easily drop into your projects. Many components are graphic user interface widgets, such as radio buttons, pull-down menus, and preload bars. But some components, such as timers, server connection utilities, or custom XML parsers, contain no graphics at all.

Flash MX components evolved from Flash 5's Smart Clips, which were movie clip symbols that allowed their variables (a.k.a. "clip parameters") to be set via the authoring tool. Typically (although not compulsorily), Flash MX components are subclasses of the built-in *MovieClip* class, giving them all the properties and methods of *MovieClip* in addition to their own properties and methods.

From a traditional Flash point of view, components are simply ready-made movie clips that can be installed into a movie's Library and then placed on the Stage. From a traditional programmer's point of view, components are building blocks that can be added to an application visually or programmatically and then wired into the application's logic and data.

Strategically, Flash MX components are Macromedia's effort to provide visual programmers with a drag-n-drop development environment, much like, say, Microsoft Visual Basic. Using components, you can create a user interface visually in the Flash authoring tool and then easily hook that interface up to routines that perform some action.

To learn how to use components to create an application GUI, see:

Introduction to Components Tutorial
> In the Flash MX authoring tool, select Help → Tutorials → Introduction to Components.

Using Components
> In the Flash MX authoring tool, select Help → Using Flash → Using Components.

Building an Address Book with Components (by your humble author)

See the web site *http://www.macromedia.com/desdev/mx/flash/articles/addressbook.html*.

Creating Forms with Components in Macromedia Flash MX

See the web site *http://www.macromedia.com/support/flash/applications/creating_forms/*.

Developers can extend Flash by creating their own custom components. For details, see Chapters 14 and 16 of *Action-Script for Flash MX: The Definitive Guide* and the following Macromedia technotes:

• How to Build a Flash MX Component: *http://www.macromedia.com/desdev/mx/flash/articles/create_components.html*

• Creating Components: *http://www.macromedia.com/support/flash/applications/creating_comps/*

The following sites have plenty of free components for download. You'll need the Macromedia Extension Manager to install components (which are distributed as *.mxp* files). You can get the Extension Manager at the Macromedia Flash Exchange (the first URL).

• *http://www.macromedia.com/exchange/flash/*

• *http://www.flashcomponents.net/*

• *http://componenthq.entclosure.com/*

Working with External Media and Data

ActionScript can load *.swf* files, images, sounds, HTML documents, variables, and XML into the Flash Player. When used with Macromedia Flash Remoting MX or Macromedia Flash Communication Server MX, Flash can even transfer serialized objects to and from external sources. (See the web sites *http://macromedia.com/software/flashremoting/* and *http://macromedia.com/software/flashcom/*.)

Loading Images and .swf Files

To load a *.swf* file into a movie clip, use the *MovieClip. loadMovie()* method:

```
someClip.loadMovie("someMovie.swf");
```

To load a *.swf* file into a document level, use the global *loadMovieNum()* function:

```
// Load a movie into document level 3
loadMovieNum("someMovie.swf", 3);
```

The *loadMovie()* method and *loadMovieNum()* function can also load nonprogressive *.jpg* files. The following code creates a container movie clip (image_mc) in the current clip (this) and loads a JPEG image (*photo.jpg*) into it:

```
this.createEmptyMovieClip("image_mc", 1);
this.image_mc.loadMovie("photo.jpg");
```

You can download an image loader/viewer class with pan and zoom features from *http://www.moock.org/asdg/codedepot/*. For information on creating load progress bars for loading *.swf* files, see *http://design.oreilly.com/news/action_0501.html*.

Loading Sounds

To load a sound, first create a *Sound* instance, then invoke its *loadSound()* method with the following arguments:

- The URL of the sound to load (MP3 files only)
- A Boolean indicating whether the sound should stream (true) or not (false)

Streamed sounds begin playback automatically as soon as the required buffer has loaded, while their counterparts, *event sounds*, must be manually started with the *Sound.start()* method after they have fully loaded.

The following code loads and plays an event sound. It uses the *Sound.onLoad()* event handler property to ensure the sound has loaded before it plays:

```
// Create a Sound object
music = new Sound();

// Define an onLoad() callback function for
// our object. (Do this before loading!)
music.onLoad = function () {
  // Place code here to respond to sound
  // load completion.
  trace("Sound has fully loaded");
  // It's an event sound and it's fully
  // loaded, so we can safely play it now
  this.start();
}

// Load the sound (second argument is
// false, so this is an event sound).
music.loadSound("http://www.somesite.com/song.mp3",
        false);
```

The next example loads the same sound as a streaming sound. The sound starts playing automatically when it has been buffered sufficiently, so no *onLoad()* handler is required:

```
// Create a Sound object
music = new Sound();
// Load the sound (second argument is true,
// so this is a streaming sound).
music.loadSound("http://www.somesite.com/song.mp3",
        true);
```

You can download a sound preloader with a load progress bar from *http://www.moock.org/asdg/codedepot/*.

Loading Web Pages

To load an HTML document or other file into the current frame or window of a web browser, use the *getURL()* function:

```
getURL("http://www.oreilly.com/");
```

The *getURL()* function launches a new browser if the Flash movie is running in the standalone version of the Player. But if the Flash movie is running in a browser, the *getURL()* function replaces the current HTML page containing the Flash Player, effectively terminating the Flash movie. To load a document into a different window or frame, supply the window or frame name as the second argument to *getURL()*. For example:

```
// Load into named frame
getURL("http://moock.org/", "contentFrame");
// Load into new window
getURL("http://moock.org/", "_blank");
```

Loading Variables

To load URL-encoded variables from a text file or server-side application, create an instance of the *LoadVars* class and invoke its *load()* method. When the variables have been received, they will be made available as properties of the instance.

For example, to retrieve the msg1 variable from the text file *vars.txt*, which looks like this:

```
msg1=hello+world
```

use the following code:

```
// Make a text field in which to display
// the loaded variable.
this.createTextField("msg1_txt", 1, 200, 200, 100, 20);

// Create the LoadVars instance.
var externalVars = new LoadVars();

// Assign an onLoad() callback to tell us
// that the variable has arrived. Do this
// before invoking load()!
externalVars.onLoad = function () {
  // When the variable arrives, display it in our
  // text field. Notice that the loaded msg1 variable
  // is accessible as a property of the externalVars
  // instance (this).
```

```
    msg1_txt.text = this.msg1;
}

// Now load the text file from the specified URL.
externalVars.load("http://www.site.com/vars.txt");
```

To prevent browsers from caching variables, append a dummy variable with a unique value to the URL:

```
externalVars.load(
"http://www.site.com/vars.txt?cacheKiller="
+ new Date().getTime());
```

To send variables to a script and receive variables back, use the *LoadVars.sendAndLoad()* method. To send variables to a script and display the results in a new browser window, use the *LoadVars.send()* method. To load variables in Flash 5 (which did not support the *LoadVars* class), use the *loadVariables()* global function.

You can download a variable preloader that shows load progress from *http://www.moock.org/asdg/codedepot/*.

Loading XML

To load XML source code from a text file or server-side application, create an instance of the *XML* class and invoke its *load()* method. When the XML has been received, it will be parsed and converted to an object hierarchy that can be accessed with the methods of the *XML* class.

For example, to retrieve XML source from the file *doc.xml*, which looks like this:

```
<P>Hello world</P>
```

use the following code:

```
// Make a text field in which to display
// the contents of the <P> tag.
this.createTextField("output_txt", 1, 200, 200, 100, 20);

// Create the XML instance.
var doc = new XML();
```

```
// Assign an onLoad() callback to tell us that the
// XML has arrived. Do this before invoking load()!
doc.onLoad = function () {
  // When the XML arrives, display the
  // contents of the <P> tag.
  output_txt.text = this.firstChild.firstChild.nodeValue;
}

// Now load the XML file from the specified URL.
doc.load("http://www.site.com/doc.xml");
```

To send XML to a script and receive XML in return, use the *XML.sendAndLoad()* method. To send XML to a script and display the results in a new browser window, use the *XML. send()* method.

You can download an XML preloader that shows load progress from *http://www.moock.org/asdg/codedepot/*.

Persistent Socket Connections

Flash can open a persistent TCP/IP socket connection to a server using either Macromedia's Flash Communication Server MX software or the *XMLSocket* class. Flash Communication Server applications support two-way data, video, and audio transfer and require Macromedia's server software. *XMLSocket* applications support two-way data transfer only (normally in XML format) and require the use of custom-built socket server software. Both types of applications support multiuser environments such as online games, chat, and shared whiteboards.

Table 11 lists both free and commercial *XMLSocket* servers.

Table 11. XMLSocket servers

Name	License	Location
moockComm	Free	*http://www.moock.org/chat/moockComm.zip*
aquaServer	Free	*http://www.figleaf.com/development/flash5/ aquaserver.zip*
Unity	Pay (free for 10 users)	*http://www.moock.org/unity*

Table 11. XMLSocket servers (continued)

Name	License	Location
Fortress	Pay	*http://www.xadra.com/products/main.html*
ElectroServer	Pay	*http://www.electrotank.com/ElectroServer*

Security Restrictions

Although security limitations have been part of the Flash Player since Version 4, Flash 6 formalizes the concept of the *security sandbox*. Under the rules of the sandbox, a movie hosted at one domain cannot:

- Invoke methods or functions in a movie loaded from another domain
- Access data (user-defined variables, user-defined properties, and nested movie clips) in a movie loaded from another domain
- Load XML or variables from another domain via the *LoadVars* class, *loadVariables( )*, *XML.load( )*, or *XML. sendAndLoad( )*
- Connect to an *XMLSocket* server on another domain

By default, the security sandbox is active and all attempts to perform the above operations are ignored by Flash Player 6. For information on overriding these restrictions, see *System. security.allowDomain( )* in *ActionScript for Flash MX: The Definitive Guide*, and the following Macromedia tech notes:

- *http://www.macromedia.com/support/flash/ts/documents/ loadvars_security.htm*
- *http://www.macromedia.com/support/flash/ts/documents/ load_xdomain.htm*

For general information on Flash security, see *http://www. macromedia.com/desdev/security/*.

Working with Web Browsers

To embed a Flash movie in a web page, use the HTML <EMBED> and <OBJECT> tags together as follows (attributes whose values are typically customized for each movie are shown in bold):

```
<OBJECT
  CLASSID="clsid:D27CDB6E-AE6D-11cf-96B8-444553540000"
  CODEBASE=
"http://download.macromedia.com/pub/shockwave/cabs/flash/
swflash.cab#version=6,0,0,0"
  WIDTH="550"
  HEIGHT="400"
  ID="main"
  ALIGN="">
  <PARAM NAME="movie" VALUE="main.swf">
  <PARAM NAME="quality" VALUE="high">
  <PARAM NAME="bgcolor" VALUE="#FFFFFF">

    <EMBED
      SRC="main.swf"
      QUALITY="high"
      BGCOLOR="#FFFFFF"
      WIDTH="550"
      HEIGHT="400"
      NAME="main"
      ALIGN=""
      TYPE="application/x-shockwave-flash"

PLUGINSPAGE="http://www.macromedia.com/go/getflashplayer">
    </EMBED>
</OBJECT>
```

In the Flash authoring tool, you can use the File → Publish command to generate <EMBED> and <OBJECT> tags automatically. For instructions, see Help → Using Flash → Publishing → Publishing Flash Documents.

The supported <EMBED> and <OBJECT> tag attributes are listed in the following tables. See also *http://www.macromedia.com/support/flash/ts/documents/tag_attributes.htm*.

Table 12 lists attributes unique to the `<OBJECT>` tag.

Table 12. `<OBJECT>` tag attributes

Attribute	Description
CLASSID	Identifier for the Flash ActiveX control.
CODEBASE	Location of the Flash ActiveX control.
ID	Identification string used by scripts to manipulate the Flash movie.
MOVIE	Location of the movie (*.swf* file).

Table 13 lists attributes unique to the `<EMBED>` tag.

Table 13. `<EMBED>` tag attributes

Attribute	Description
NAME	Identification string used by scripts to manipulate the Flash movie.
PLUGINSPAGE	Location of the Flash plugin on Macromedia's web site.
SRC	Location of the movie (*.swf* file).
SWLIVECONNECT	When `true`, the browser loads Java when loading the Flash Player for the first time. Defaults to `false`. Required by movies controlled by JavaScript.
TYPE	The MIME content type for Flash.

Table 14 lists attributes common to the `<EMBED>` and `<OBJECT>` tags.

Table 14. Common `<EMBED>` and `<OBJECT>` tag attributes

Attribute	Description
ALIGN	Positions the movie in the browser window. Values are: `""` (centered), `"LEFT"`, `"RIGHT"`, `"TOP"`, or `"BOTTOM"`.
BASE	URL to use as the base of all relative URLs in the movie.
BGCOLOR	Background color of the movie.
HEIGHT	Height of the movie in pixels or as a percentage of the HTML page height.
LOOP	Causes the Flash animation to loop continuously (if `true`, the default) or stop when the playhead reaches the end of the movie (if `false`).
MENU	Indicates whether the Flash Player's contextual menu contains a full list of items (if `true`, the default) or a minimal list of items (if `false`).

Table 14. Common <EMBED> and <OBJECT> tag attributes

Attribute	Description
PLAY	When `true` (the default), the movie plays immediately upon loading.
QUALITY	Sets the antialiasing level of text and graphics. Values are: `"BEST"`, `"HIGH"`, `"AUTOHIGH"`, `"MEDIUM"`, `"AUTOLOW"`, or `"LOW"`.
SALIGN	Dictates the positioning of the movie relative to the space available to the Flash Player. See `Stage.align` in the reference section.
SCALE	Controls scaling. Values are: `"EXACTFIT"`, `"NOBORDER"`, `"NOSCALE"`, or `"SHOWALL"`. See `Stage.scaleMode` in the reference section.
WIDTH	Width of the movie in pixels or as a percentage of the HTML page width.
WMODE	Lets Flash movies use DHTML's layering, absolute positioning, and transparency features (supported browsers only). Values are: `"WINDOW"` (the default), `"OPAQUE"`, or `"TRANSPARENT"`.

JavaScript Communication

In some browsers, Flash movies can invoke JavaScript functions using the *fscommand()* function or the `javascript:` protocol of a *getURL()* function. Conversely, JavaScript can control a Flash movie using the Flash Methods. For documentation and examples, see *http://www.moock.org/webdesign/flash/fscommand/*.

Finding Help, Examples, and Code Libraries

For tech notes on specific ActionScript topics, see:

- *http://www.macromedia.com/support/flash*
- *http://www.moock.org/asdg/technotes*

For downloadable code samples and libraries, see:

- *http://www.macromedia.com/exchange/flash*
- *http://www.layer51.com/proto*
- *http://www.moock.org/asdg/codedepot*

For online community lists, see:

- *http://chattyfig.figleaf.com*
- *http://www.were-here.com*
- *http://www.ultrashock.com*

For general ActionScript resources, see:

- *http://www.flashkit.com*
- *http://www.actionscript.org*
- *http://www.actionscript.com*

ActionScript Language Reference

The remainder of this book provides quick-reference coverage of the core classes and objects of ActionScript and briefly describes their purpose, properties, methods, and event handlers. Table 15 lists the core classes and objects.

Table 15. Core ActionScript classes and objects

Accessibility	LoadVars	Stage
Arguments	LocalConnection	String
Array	Math	System
Boolean	Mouse	TextField
Button	MovieClip	TextFormat
Capabilities	Number	XML
Color	Object	XMLnode
Date	Selection	XMLSocket
Function	SharedObject	
Key	Sound	

Table 16 lists the *global functions*, which are available throughout any movie. It also lists ActionScript's pragmas (#endinitclip and #initclip) and directive (#include).

Table 16. ActionScript global functions, pragmas, and directives

Boolean( )	isFinite( )	random( )
call( )	isNaN( )	removeMovieClip( )
clearInterval( )	loadMovie( )	setInterval( )
Date( )	loadMovieNum( )	setProperty( )
duplicateMovieClip( )	loadVariables( )	startDrag( )
#endinitclip	loadVariablesNum( )	stop( )
escape( )	nextFrame( )	stopAllSounds( )
eval( )	nextScene( )	stopDrag( )
fscommand( )	Number( )	String( )
getProperty( )	parseFloat( )	targetPath( )
getTimer( )	parseInt( )	tellTarget( )
getURL( )	play( )	toggleHighQuality( )
getVersion( )	prevFrame( )	trace( )
gotoAndPlay( )	prevScene( )	unescape( )
gotoAndStop( )	print( )	unloadMovie( )
#include	printAsBitmap( )	unloadMovieNum( )
#initclip	printAsBitmapNum( )	updateAfterEvent( )
int( )	printNum( )	

Table 17 lists ActionScript's global properties, which are available throughout any movie.

Table 17. ActionScript global properties

_focusrect	NaN
_global	_quality
_highquality	_root
Infinity	_soundbuftime
-Infinity	$version
_leveln	

tools for developing advanced accessible UI components

```
Accessibility.propertyName
Accessibility.methodName()
```

The *Accessibility* object manages communication between the Flash Player and screen readers or accessibility aids such as GW Micro's Window-Eyes (*http://www.gwmicro.com*). At the time of this writing, the Macromedia ActionScript Component Accessibility API works with Microsoft Active Accessibility (MSAA) only; hence, only the ActiveX version of Flash Player 6 supports communication with an external accessibility application.

For more information on accessibility in Flash, see *http://www. macromedia.com/macromedia/accessibility/features/flash/*.

Properties

_accProps

> An object whose properties specify accessibility information for screen readers. May be global or attached to a specific object instance. Supported _accProps properties are silent, forceSimple, name, description, and shortcut. Added in Flash Player 6.0.65.0. See *http://www.macromedia.com/support/ flash/releasenotes/player/rn_6.html*.

Methods

isActive()

> Returns true if an accessibility aid program (generally a screen reader) is communicating with the Flash Player.

sendEvent(movieClip, childID, event, isNonHtml)

> Sends an event notice to Microsoft Active Accessibility (MSAA).

updateProperties()

> Refreshes the descriptions and accessibility properties of all objects (as set via _accProps); sends changes to active screen readers. Added in Flash Player 6.0.65.0.

Arguments Object Flash 5; caller property added in Flash 6

access to function arguments, the current function, and the calling function

```
arguments[elem]
arguments.propertyName
```

The *Arguments* object is stored in the local `arguments` variable of every function and is accessible only while a function is executing. `arguments[0]` is the first passed parameter, `arguments[1]` is the second passed parameter, and so on. As of Flash 6, arguments supports all *Array* methods and properties (*pop()*, *shift()*, etc.); prior to Flash 6, arguments supported the `length` property, but not the *Array* methods.

Properties

callee
    A reference to the function being executed.

caller
    A reference to the calling function.

length
    The number of arguments passed to the function being executed.

Array Class Flash 5; sortOn( ) method added in Flash 6

array creation and manipulation

Constructor

```
new Array()       // empty array
new Array(len)    // array with len undefined elements
new Array(element0, ...elementn)  // specified elements
```

Properties

length
    The number of elements in an array (including empty elements).

Array Class | 65

Methods

concat(value1, ...valuen)

Creates a new array by appending additional elements to an existing array.

join(delimiter)

Converts the elements of an array into a string concatenated with an optional delimiter (defaults to comma).

pop()

Removes and returns the last element of an array, decrementing the array length.

push(value1, ...valuen)

Adds one or more elements to the end of an array, and returns the new length of the array.

reverse()

Reverses the order of elements in an array.

shift()

Removes and returns the first element of an array.

slice(startIndex, endIndex)

Creates a new array containing elements from *startIndex* up to, but not including, *endIndex*. Indexes are zero-relative.

sort(compareFunction)

Sorts the elements of an array according to Unicode code points or using an optional *compareFunction*. Your custom *compareFunction* should return a negative number if the first element should come before the second element; a positive number if the first element should come after the second element; or 0 if the elements should not be reordered.

sortOn(key)

Sorts an array of objects by the property name specified by the string *key*.

splice(startIndex, deleteCount, value1, ...valuen)

Deletes the specified number of array elements starting at *startIndex*, then inserts the remaining arguments into the array. It returns an array containing the deleted elements.

toString()

Converts an array to a string of comma-separated element values.

---

unshift(value1, ...valuen)
> Adds one or more elements to the beginning of an array and
> returns the new length of the array.

See Also   *String.split()*

Boolean( ) Function

convert a value to the boolean datatype

Boolean(*value*)

Converts value to a Boolean (either true or false). See Table 6.

Boolean Class

wrapper class for primitive Boolean data

Constructor

new Boolean(*value*)

Methods

toString()
> Returns a string ("true" or "false") depending on the value of
> a *Boolean* object.

valueOf()
> Returns the primitive Boolean value of the object (true or
> false).

Button Class

control over buttons in a movie

Constructor

None. *Button* objects must be created manually in the authoring
tool. Use movie clips to simulate runtime-generated buttons. You
should use the provided *Up*, *Over*, and *Down* frames in the
authoring tool to create highlight states for buttons.

Properties

_alpha
> Opacity percentage: 0 is transparent; 100 is opaque.

enabled
> Boolean; allows or disallows mouse interaction. A disabled button can still receive keyboard focus with the Tab key unless the tabEnabled property is also false.

_focusrect
> Boolean; enables or disables automatic yellow highlight rectangle surrounding a button when it receives keyboard focus. If set to null (the default), Flash uses the value of the global _focusrect property.

_height
> Height of the button, in pixels. This can differ for its *Up*, *Over*, and *Down* states.

_name
> Returns the instance name of the *Button* object specified in the Property inspector during authoring, as a string.

_parent
> A reference to the movie clip in which the button resides.

_rotation
> Clockwise rotation, in degrees, of the button.

tabEnabled
> Boolean; includes or excludes the button from the current tab order.

tabIndex
> An integer specifying the button's index in the custom tab order. When at least one object has tabIndex set, any object with no assigned tabIndex cannot be accessed via the Tab key.

_target
> The target path of the button, in a Flash 4–style slash notation string.

trackAsMenu
> Modifies the button's *onRelease()* handler requirements, enabling menu-style behavior. When trackAsMenu is true, releasing the mouse over a button triggers its *onRelease()* handler, unless the mouse was originally pressed over a button for which trackAsMenu is false or undefined. The trackAsMenu property should be set the same for all buttons in a menu; otherwise, mayhem and confusion can ensue.

_url

> The network URL of the movie clip that contains the button, as a string.

useHandCursor

> Boolean; dictates whether a hand icon is displayed when the mouse is over the button. See *Mouse.hide()*.

_visible

> Boolean; controls whether the button is shown or hidden. Invisible buttons can still be controlled via ActionScript, but they are not visible on screen and cannot receive user events.

_width

> Width of the button, in pixels. This can differ for its *Up*, *Over*, and *Down* states.

_x Horizontal location of the button's registration point, in pixels, relative to the Stage's left edge (or relative to the parent movie clip's registration point).

_xmouse

> Horizontal location of the mouse pointer's hotspot, in pixels, relative to the button's registration point.

_xscale

> Width of the button, as a percentage of the original width of its Library symbol.

_y Vertical location of the button's registration point, in pixels, relative to the Stage's top edge (or relative to the parent movie clip's registration point)

_ymouse

> Vertical location of the mouse pointer's hotspot, in pixels, relative to the button's registration point.

_yscale

> Height of the button, as a percentage of the original height of its Library symbol.

Methods

getDepth()

> Returns the integer depth of the button in the content stack, in the range of −116383 to −1. Objects on higher depths appear in front of those with lower depths.

Event Handlers

on(keyPress key)

The event handler triggered when the specified key is pressed. The *key* can be a letter, such as "a", or one of: "<Delete>", "<Down>", "<End>", "<Enter>", "<Home>", "<Insert>", "<Left>", "<PgDn>", "<PgUp>", "<Right>", "<Space>", "<Tab>", "<Up>". In Flash 6, *Key.onKeyUp()* and *Key.onKeyDown()* are the preferred keyboard-handling tools. The *on(keyPress)* event is not available in event handler property form.

onDragOut()

Occurs when the mouse is clicked while the pointer is over a Flash button and then the pointer moves off the Flash button without the mouse button being released.

onDragOver()

Occurs when the mouse is clicked while the pointer is over a Flash button and then the pointer moves off and back onto the Flash button without the mouse button being released.

onKillFocus(newFocus)

Occurs when the button loses focus. The *newFocus* parameter represents the *TextField*, *MovieClip*, or *Button* object that now has focus, or null if no object has received focus. See *Selection.setFocus()*.

onPress()

Occurs when the mouse is clicked while the pointer is over a Flash button.

onRelease()

Occurs when the mouse is pressed and then released while the pointer is over a Flash button. See `Button.trackAsMenu`.

onReleaseOutside()

Occurs when the mouse is clicked over the Flash button and then released after rolling off the button.

onRollOut()

Occurs when the pointer moves off the Flash button (while the mouse is not depressed).

onRollOver()

Occurs when the pointer moves over the Flash button (while the mouse is not depressed) or when the button gains keyboard focus.

onSetFocus(oldFocus)

Occurs when the Flash button gains focus. The *oldFocus* parameter represents the *TextField*, *MovieClip*, or *Button* object that previously had focus, or null if no object was previously focused.

call( )

execute the script of a remote frame

call(*frameNumberOrLabel*)

The *call()* function executes the script at the specified frame number or frame label. As of Flash 5, you should declare and invoke ActionScript functions instead of executing remote frame scripts via *call()*.

Capabilities Object

information about the Flash Player and its host system

System.capabilities.*propertyName*

The *Capabilities* object represents the specifications of the Flash Player and the system on which the Player is running. It is stored as a property of the *System* object (i.e., System.capabilities). Hence, references to *Capabilities* properties always start with the *System* object, as follows:

System.capabilities.*propertyName*

All properties of *Capabilities* have corresponding short-form names and values that can be used to convey the client-side Player's abilities to a server-side script. The serverString property joins all short-form property name/value pairs into a URL-encoded string suitable for transmission to a server. Possible values for Boolean properties in the server string are t (true) and f (false); others are as noted in the following descriptions.

Properties

hasAccessibility

Boolean indicating whether the Player supports Microsoft Active Accessibility (MSAA). Corresponding server string is ACC.

hasAudio

> Boolean indicating whether the Player supports audio play-
> back, not whether the computer actually has audio enabled
> (i.e., has a sound card, speakers turned on, volume on, etc.).
> Corresponding server string is A.

hasAudioEncoder

> Boolean indicating whether the system can encode audio.
> Corresponding server string is AE.

hasMP3

> Boolean indicating whether the Player supports MP3 sound
> playback. Corresponding server string is MP3.

hasVideoEncoder

> Boolean indicating whether the system can encode video, not
> whether the necessary hardware (such as a webcam) is
> present. Corresponding server string is VE.

input

> The user input device for the system, such as a mouse (indi-
> cated by the word "point"). Corresponding server string is I.

isDebugger

> Boolean indicating whether the Player is a debugging version.
> Corresponding server string is DEB.

language

> The current language setting on the operating system, as a
> two-letter code (e.g., "en" for English, "fr" for French, "ja" for
> Japanese, "ko" for Korean, "de" for German, and "es" for
> Spanish) as specified at *http://lcweb.loc.gov/standards/iso639-
> 2/englangn.html*. The language code can also include a
> hyphen and a two-letter country code (e.g., "en-US" for
> American English, "en-UK" for British English, "zh-CN" for
> Simplified Chinese, and "zh-TW" for Traditional Chinese).
> Corresponding server string is LAN.

manufacturer

> The creator of the Player. For the desktop version of the Flash
> Player, the only values are "Macromedia Windows" and
> "Macromedia Macintosh". Corresponding server string is M.

os

> The operating system on which the Player is running, such as
> "Windows XP", "Windows 2000", "Windows NT",

"Windows 98/ME", "Windows 95", or "Windows CE". On Macintosh, os returns "MacOS *x.y.z*", such as "MacOS 9.2.1" or "MacOS 10.1.4". Corresponding server string is OS.

pixelAspectRatio

The width-to-height ratio of a pixel on the screen, such as 1.0. Corresponding server string is AR.

screenColor

The color mode supported by the screen. Possible values are "color" (supports more than two colors), "gray" (grayscale), and "bw" (black and white or two-color display). Corresponding server string is COL.

screenDPI

The number of pixels per linear inch displayed by the screen, typically 72. Corresponding server string is DP.

screenResolutionX

The width of the screen, in pixels, analogous to JavaScript's Screen.width property. See also Stage.width. Corresponding server string is R, with a value that includes both the width and height of the screen, formatted as "*WIDTHxHEIGHT*" (for example, "1600x1200").

screenResolutionY

The height of the screen, in pixels, analogous to JavaScript's Screen.height property. See also Stage.height. See screenResolutionX for server string details.

serverString

All *Capabilities* properties and values, as a URL-encoded string, such as:

```
"A=t&MP3=t&AE=t&VE=t&ACC=f&DEB=t&V=WIN%206%2C0%2C21%2C
0&M=Macromedia
Windows&R=1600x1200&DP=72&COL=color&AR=1.
0&I=point&OS=Windows XP&L=en"
```

version

The Flash Player version of the form *platform major,minor,build,patch*. For example: "WIN 6,0,23,0", "MAC 5,0,41,0", "UNIX 4,0,12,0". Corresponding server string is V. See also *getVersion()* and $version. For plugin-sniffing code, see *http://www.moock.org/webdesign/flash/detection/moockfpi/*.

clearInterval( )   Flash 6

stop the periodic execution of a function or method

```
clearInterval(intervalID)
```

The *setInterval()* and *clearInterval()* functions are used to create
and destroy *intervals*, which execute a specified function or object
method periodically. An interval is created by calling *setInterval()*,
which returns a unique identifier that can later be passed to
clearInterval() to halt the interval.

Color Class   Flash 5

control over movie clip color values

Constructor

```
new Color(target)
```

Description

We use objects of the *Color* class to dictate the color and transparency of a movie clip or main movie programmatically. Once we've
created an object of the *Color* class for a specific *target*, we can
then invoke the methods of that *Color* object to affect its *target*'s
color and transparency.

Colors are defined by four separate components: Red, Green, Blue,
and Alpha (or transparency), each in the range of 0 to 255. RGB
colors are typically specified as a hexadecimal triplet of the form
0x*RRGGBB*, where *RR*, *GG*, and *BB* are each two-digit hex numbers
representing Red, Green, and Blue. For example, pure red can be
expressed as 0xFF0000. This code makes the main movie red:

```
var c = new Color(_root);
c.setRGB(0xFF0000);
```

Manual color transformations can be applied to movie clips in the
Flash MX authoring tool via the Property inspector. Manual transformations are merged with runtime transformations according to
the following calculations:

```
R = originalRed   * (redPercent/100)   + redOffset
G = originalGreen * (greenPercent/100) + greenOffset
B = originalBlue  * (bluePercent/100)  + blueOffset
A = originalAlpha * (alphaPercent/100) + alphaOffset
```

Methods

getRGB( )

Returns an integer from –16777215 to 16777215 representing the current offset values for Red, Green, and Blue components of the target clip's color. Color offsets are most easily read using *getTransform( )*, which returns each component separately.

getTransform( )

Returns a transform object whose properties indicate the current Red, Green, Blue, and Alpha offsets (rb, gb, bb, and ab), ranging from –255 to 255, and percentages (ra, ga, ba, and aa), ranging from –100 to 100.

setRGB(offset)

Assigns new offset values for Red, Green, and Blue, while setting percentage values to 0. The *offset* is a number in the range 0 to 16777215 but is most easily specified as a six-digit hexadecimal number from 0x000000 to 0xFFFFFF.

setTransform(transformObject)

Assigns new offset and/or percentage values for Red, Green, Blue, and Alpha using a transform object that defines the properties described under *getTransform( )*.

See Also   MovieClip._alpha

Date( )   Flash 5

a string representing the current date and time

Date( )

The *Date( )* function returns a human-readable string that expresses the current date and local time. The string also includes the GMT offset (the number of hours difference between local time and Greenwich Mean Time).

current time and structured support for date information

Constructor

```
new Date()
new Date(milliseconds)
new Date(year, month, day, hours, minutes, seconds, ms)
```

Description

Objects of the *Date* class can determine the current time and date, and can store arbitrary dates and times in a structured format. In ActionScript, a specific date is represented by the number of milliseconds before or after midnight of January 1, 1970. There are three ways to make a new *Date* object:

- Invoke the *Date()* constructor with no arguments. This sets the new *Date* object to the current time.

- Invoke the *Date()* constructor with one numeric argument: the number of milliseconds between midnight, January 1, 1970 and the date you're creating.

- Invoke the *Date()* constructor with two to seven numeric arguments: the year and month (mandatory) and (optionally) the day, hour, minute, second, and millisecond of the date you're creating.

When *Date()* is used as a global function—without the new keyword—it generates a string that expresses the current time in the same format as would be returned by *Date.toString()*.

Class Methods

UTC(year, month, day, hours, minutes, seconds, ms)
    Returns the number of milliseconds between January 1, 1970 and a supplied UTC date. The *Date.UTC()* method takes the same arguments as the *Date()* constructor, but instead of returning a *Date* object for the specified date, *Date.UTC()* returns a number indicating the date in the internal milliseconds-from-1970 format (useful for passing to *setTime()*).

Methods

Some methods are listed as variants that differ for local and UTC time. For example, *get[UTC]Date()* means that *getDate()* retrieves the day of the specified *Date* object in local time, and *getUTCDate()* retrieves the day in UTC (universal) time. The "setter" methods, such as *setDate()*, return an integer representing the number of milliseconds between the new date and midnight, January 1, 1970.

get[UTC]Date()

Returns the day of the month from 1 to 31.

get[UTC]Day()

Returns the day of the week as a number from 0 (Sunday) to 6 (Saturday).

get[UTC]FullYear()

Returns the four-digit year.

get[UTC]Hours()

Returns the hour, from 0 (midnight) to 23 (11 P.M.).

get[UTC]Milliseconds()

Returns the milliseconds (i.e., the fractional remainder of the seconds indicated by the specified *Date* object), from 0 to 999. Use *getTime()* to retrieve the number of milliseconds since 1970.

get[UTC]Minutes()

Returns the minutes, from 0 to 59.

get[UTC]Month()

Returns the month of the year as a number from 0 (January) to 11 (December), not 1 to 12.

get[UTC]Seconds()

Returns the seconds, from 0 to 59.

getTime()

Returns the date in internal format (i.e., the number of milliseconds between January 1, 1970 and the time of a *Date* object).

getTimezoneOffset()

Returns the number of minutes between UTC and local time.

getYear( )

    Returns the year, relative to 1900. For example, 1999 is returned as 99, 2001 is returned as 101, and 1800 is returned as −100.

set[UTC]Date(day)

    Assigns the day of the month, as an integer from 1 to 31.

set[UTC]FullYear(year, month, day)

    Assigns the century and year in four-digit format. The month and day are optional and default to 0 (i.e., January) and 1.

set[UTC]Hours(hour)

    Assigns the hour of the day, from 0 (midnight) to 23 (11 P.M.).

set[UTC]Milliseconds(ms)

    Assigns the milliseconds (i.e., the fractional remainder of the seconds indicated by the specified *Date* object), from 0 to 999. Use *setTime( )* to assign the number of milliseconds since 1970.

set[UTC]Minutes(minutes)

    Assigns the minutes, from 0 to 59.

set[UTC]Month(month)

    Assigns the month as an integer from 0 (January) to 11 (December), not from 1 to 12.

set[UTC]Seconds(seconds)

    Assigns the seconds, from 0 to 59.

setTime(milliseconds)

    Assigns the date in internal format (i.e., the number of milliseconds since January 1, 1970).

setYear(year, month, day)

    Assigns the year in four-digit format, or in two-digit format for the twentieth century. *setYear( )* is identical to *setFullYear( )* except that it interprets one- and two-digit years as being relative to 1900, whereas *setFullYear( )* interprets them as being relative to 0 A.D.

toString( )

    A human-readable string, such as "Wed Sep 15 12:11:33 GMT-0400 1999", representing the date.

---

valueOf()

Returns the number of milliseconds between midnight of January 1, 1970 UTC and the time of the *Date* object. (In practice, this is the same as *Date.getTime()*.)

See Also   *clearInterval()*, *getTimer()*, *setInterval()*

delete Operator
Flash 5

delete the contents of a variable, property, or array element

```
delete identifier
```

The *delete* operator removes an object, an object property, an array element's contents, or a variable from a script. It returns true if the *identifier* was deleted, false if not (because the *identifier* doesn't exist or its value cannot be deleted).

duplicateMovieClip( )
Flash 4

create a copy of a movie clip

```
duplicateMovieClip(target, newName, depth)
```

#endinitclip Pragma
Flash 6

end a movie clip initialization code block begun with #initclip

```
#endinitclip
```

escape( )
Flash 5; enhanced to support UTF-8 in Flash 6

encode a string for safe network transfer

```
escape(string)
```

The *escape()* function creates a new encoded string based on a supplied string. The new string contains a hexadecimal escape sequence in place of any character in the supplied string that is not a digit or a basic unaccented Latin letter between A and Z or a and z. To decode an encoded string, use the global *unescape()* function.

eval( ) Flash 4; illegal on left side of assignment in Flash 6

interpret a string as an identifier

eval(*stringExpression*)

The *eval()* function provides a means of dynamically constructing an identifier based on a string of text. It looks up the variable identified by *stringExpression* and returns its value.

_focusrect Flash 4

enable or disable automatic highlight on keyboard-focused buttons and clips   read/write

_focusrect

When a button has keyboard focus, Flash places a yellow rectangle around that button. You can turn off the yellow rectangle by setting the _focusrect global property to false. This property can be overridden for individual button or movie clip instances via *Button.*_focusrect and *MovieClip.*_focusrect.

fscommand( ) Flash 3; enhanced in Flash 5 to support "trapallkeys"

send a message to the Player's host application

fscommand(*command, parameters*)

The *fscommand()* function is used to send commands to the Standalone Player (see Table 18) or to the application hosting the Flash Player, such as a web browser.

Table 18. Command/argument pairs in Standalone Player

Command	Argument	Description
"allowscale"	"true" or "false"	Stage.scaleMode is preferred.
"exec"	"application_name"	Launches an external application. In Flash MX, the application must reside in a folder named *fscommand* directly beneath the *.swf* file.
"fullscreen"	"true" or "false"	When "true", causes the Standalone Player's window to maximize (fill the entire screen).
"quit"	N/A	Closes the movie and exits the Standalone Player.

Table 18. Command/argument pairs in Standalone Player

Command	Argument	Description
"showmenu"	"true" or "false"	Stage.showMenu is preferred.
"trapallkeys"	"true" or "false"	When "true", disables the control keys in the Standalone Player.

When used from within a *.swf* file playing in a browser, *fscommand()* invokes a special JavaScript function (in Netscape) or VBScript function (in Internet Explorer) on the HTML page that contains the movie. The special function name takes the form *movieID_DoFSCommand()*, where *movieID* is the name specified in the HTML <OBJECT> tag's ID attribute (in Internet Explorer) or the <EMBED> tag's NAME attribute (in Netscape). Not supported in all browsers.

Function Class

Flash 6

object-oriented representation of ActionScript functions

The *Function* class is used to store, pass, and compare functions as ActionScript data. New *Function* objects are defined with either the *function* statement or a function literal (there is no *Function* constructor).

Properties

prototype
> An object specifying methods and properties for a class. See "Object-Oriented ActionScript."

Methods

apply(thisObj, parametersArray)
> Invokes a function as an object method, passing parameters in an array, and returns result of function.

call(thisObj, param1, param2, ...paramn)
> Invokes a function as an object method, passing parameters in a comma-delimited list, and returns result of function.

toString()
> Returns a string representation of the function object.

getProperty( ) Flash 4

retrieve the value of a movie clip property

```
getProperty(movieClip, property)
```

getTimer( ) Flash 4

return the number of milliseconds that have elapsed since the Player started running

```
getTimer()
```

getURL( ) Flash 2; method parameter added in Flash 4

load a URL into a browser

```
getURL(url, window, method)
```

The *getURL()* function is used to:

- Load a document (usually a web page) into a web browser frame or window
- Execute a server-side script and receive the results in a browser frame or window
- Execute JavaScript code in a web browser
- Trigger events from Flash assets imported as sprites into Macromedia Director

See Table 19 for protocols that can be specified within the *url* parameter. The *window* parameter can be a browser window name or "_blank", "_parent", "_self", or "_top". The method parameter must be the literal "GET" or "POST".

As of Flash 6, *LoadVars.send()* is preferred over *getURL()* for sending variables to a remote server application or script and receiving results in a web browser.

Table 19. Supported protocols for getURL()

Protocol example	Purpose
"event: *eventName params*"	Send an event to Director if the Flash asset is a Director sprite.
"file:///driveSpec/folder/filename"	Access a local file.

Table 19. Supported protocols for getURL() (continued)

Protocol example	Purpose
"ftp://server.domain.com/folder/filename"	Access a remote file via FTP.
"http://server.domain.com/folder/filename"	Access a remote file via HTTP.
"javascript: *command* "	Perform JavaScript command in browser.
"lingo: *command* "	Perform Lingo command if Flash asset is a Director sprite.
"print:", "*targetClip*"	Print the target clip. In Flash 5 or later, use *print( )* instead.
"vbscript: *command* "	Perform VBScript command in browser.
"mailto:user@somedomain.com"	Send email via the default mail program on the user's system.
"telnet://domain.com:8888/"	Telnet to domain.com on port 8888.

getVersion( ) Flash 5

retrieve the platform and version of the Flash Player

getVersion( )

The *getVersion()* function returns the same string as the System.capabilities.version property but is supported in Flash 5. See the capabilities.version entry for details on its format.

_global Object Flash 6

container for global variables

_global.*variableName*

The _global object enables the creation of global variables (i.e., variables that are available from the timeline of any movie clip or level). All nonlocal variables created in ActionScript are scoped to the movie clip in which they are created. To make a variable directly accessible throughout all timelines in a movie, add it as a property to _global as follows:

```
_global.someGlobalVar = someValue;
```

gotoAndPlay( ) Flash 2

move the current timeline's playhead to a given frame and play the current clip or movie

```
gotoAndPlay(frameNumberOrLabel)
gotoAndPlay(scene, frameNumberOrLabel)
```

gotoAndStop( ) Flash 2

move the current timeline's playhead to a given frame and stop the current clip or movie

```
gotoAndStop(frameNumberOrLabel)
gotoAndStop(scene, frameNumberOrLabel)
```

_highquality Flash 4; deprecated in Flash 5 in favor of _quality

the rendering quality of the Player as an integer: 0 (Low), 1 (High), or 2 (Best)   read/write

```
_highquality
```

#include Directive Flash 5

import the text of an external ActionScript file

```
#include path
```

The #include directive imports script text from an external text file (preferably one with the *.as* extension) into the current script at compile time. It is commonly used to incorporate the same block of code in multiple scripts or across Flash projects (much as you'd use an external asset library).

Infinity Flash 5

a constant representing an infinite number   read-only

```
Infinity
```

-Infinity Flash 5

a constant representing an infinite negative number   read-only

```
-Infinity
```

#initclip Pragma

start a movie clip initialization code block

#initclip *order*

The #initclip pragma starts a special block of code that allows you to perform initialization for a movie clip symbol before any instances of it are created. Typically, it is used to create components that register a movie clip symbol with an ActionScript class (via *Object.registerClass()*). An #initclip block can appear only on frame 1 of a movie clip symbol. The #endinitclip pragma closes the #initclip block.

Use the *order* parameter to assign the #initclip block an execution priority level. Blocks with lower *order* numbers are executed before those with higher ones. Blocks without a specified *order* are executed before all numbered blocks.

NOTE

Because functions defined in an #initclip block are scoped to the _root timeline, all variable, property, and method references inside the function must be qualified explicitly.

instanceof Operator
Flash 6

returns true if the object is an instance of the specified class, and false if not

object instanceof *classConstructor*

int( )
Flash 4; deprecated in Flash 5

truncate the decimal portion of a number

int(*number*)

isFinite( )
Flash 5

returns true if a number is less than Infinity and greater than −Infinity

isFinite(*number*)

isFinite( ) | 85

isNaN( )

Flash 5

returns true if value is NaN

isNaN(*value*)

Key Object

Flash 5

determine the state of keys on the keyboard

Key.*propertyName*
Key.*methodName( )*

The *Key* object is used to detect keyboard input (i.e., the pressing and releasing of keys) and to determine the last key pressed.

Properties

Table 20 lists the properties of the *Key* object.

Table 20. Key object keycode properties

Property	Equivalent keycode	Property	Equivalent keycode
BACKSPACE	8	INSERT	45
CAPSLOCK	20	LEFT	37
CONTROL	17	PGDN	34
DELETEKEY	46	PGUP	33
DOWN	40	RIGHT	39
END	35	SHIFT	16
ENTER	13	SPACE	32
ESCAPE	27	TAB	9
HOME	36	UP	38

Methods

addListener(listener)
Registers an object to receive *onKeyUp( )* and *onKeyDown( )* events.

getAscii( )
   Returns the ASCII value of the last key pressed.

getCode( )
   Returns the keycode of the last key pressed.

isDown(keycode)
   Returns true if the specified key is currently depressed.

isToggled(keycode)
   Returns true if the Num Lock (144), Caps Lock (20), or Scroll
   Lock (145) keys are activated.

removeListener(listener)
   Cancels event notices for the specified listener. Returns true if
   removal was successful.

Listener Events

onKeyDown( )
   Occurs when a key is depressed.

onKeyUp( )
   Occurs when a key is released.

See Also   *Button   keyPress,   fscommand("trapallkeys",*
                "true"),   MovieClip.onKeyDown( ),   MovieClip.
                onKeyUp( )

_leveln   Flash 3

a document level in the Player   read-only

_level*n*

Multiple *.swf* files can be loaded into the Flash Player for simulta-
neous display. Each loaded *.swf* can be placed in a movie clip or in
its own "level" in the Flash Player's document level stack. Each
level*n* property, such as _level0, _level1, etc., stores a reference
to the main timeline of a *.swf* loaded into a document level in the
Player. The original document loaded into any Flash Player is
considered _ level0.

See Also   *loadMovie( ), _root*

loadMovie( )   Flash 4; Flash 6 adds .jpg loading and security restrictions

load an external .swf or .jpg file into the Player

```
loadMovie(url, target, method)
```

Import the *.swf* movie or *.jpg* image file located at *url* into the
target movie clip. Legal values for *method* are "GET" and "POST".

loadMovieNum( )   Flash 3; Flash 6 adds .jpg loading and security restrictions

load an external .swf or .jpg file into a document level

```
loadMovieNum(url, levelNum, method)
```

The *loadMovieNum()* function is nearly identical to *loadMovie()*
used with a document level as its *target*, except that the target
levelNum is specified as an integer (0, 1, 2, etc.) rather than as a
string.

loadVariables( )   Flash 4

retrieve an external set of variables

```
loadVariables(url, target, method)
```

The *loadVariables()* function can import variables into a movie
from a text file or a server-side application such as a Perl script.
However, as of Flash 6, the *LoadVars* class is preferred.

loadVariablesNum( )   Flash 5

attach an external set of variables to a document level

```
loadVariablesNum(url, levelNum, method)
```

The *loadVariablesNum()* function is nearly identical to
loadVariables() used with a document level as its *target*, except
that the target *levelNum* is specified as an integer (0, 1, 2, etc.)
rather than as a string.

export variables to, or import variables from, an external source

Constructor

```
new LoadVars()
```

Description

The *LoadVars* class transfers variables to or from an external source, such as a text file or a server-side script. For example:

```
var lv = new LoadVars();
lv.onLoad = function (success) {
  trace("Load succeeded? " + success);
  if (success) {
    // List loaded variables...
    for(var p in this) {
      if (p != "onLoad") {
        trace("var " + p
          + " loaded with value: " + this[p]);
      }
    }
  }
}
lv.load("http://www.site.com/theVars.txt");
```

Properties

contentType

> The MIME content type used for *send()* and *sendAndLoad()* operations.

loaded

> A Boolean; true if a *load()* or *sendAndLoad()* operation has completed.

Methods

decode(varString)

> Converts a URL-encoded string of variables to properties of the specified *LoadVars* object.

getBytesLoaded( )

Returns an integer representing the portion of loading variables that have arrived, in bytes.

getBytesTotal( )

Returns the expected total byte size of loading variables.

load(url)

Imports URL-encoded variables from a text file or a server-side application at the specified *url*.

send(url, target, method)

Transfers URL-encoded variables to a server-side application or script. The *target* parameter specifies a browser window or frame name in which to display any response sent by the script at *url*. The optional *method* is "GET" or "POST".

sendAndLoad(url, targetObject, method)

Transfers variables to a server-side application, and receives variables in return. The *targetObject* parameter specifies the *LoadVars* object that will receive the loaded variables. The optional *method* is "GET" or "POST".

toString( )

Returns the URL-encoded string of variables that would be sent by *send( )* or *sendAndLoad( )*.

Event Handlers

onData(src)

Handler executed when external variable data finishes loading but before it is parsed, where *src* is a string containing raw URL-encoded variables.

onLoad(success)

Handler executed when external variables have been converted into object properties, where *success* is true if loading was successful.

transmit data directly between movies running on the same system

Constructor

```
new LocalConnection()
```

Description

The *LocalConnection* class lets movies running in different Flash Players communicate with each other. The Players must be running on the same computer, but they can be embedded in any application. To transfer information between two Flash Players running on different machines, use *XML*, *LoadVars*, *XMLSocket*, or the Macromedia Flash Communication Server MX (Comm Server).

All *LocalConnection* applications involve at least two *LocalConnection* objects, one in the receiver (the movie that receives messages) and one in the sender (the movie that sends messages). A *LocalConnection* object can act as both a sender and a receiver, allowing two objects to engage in bidirectional communication.

Methods

close( )
> Closes an open connection to stop it from receiving messages.

connect(connectionName)
> Opens a named connection, returning true if successful.

domain( )
> Returns a string indicating the movie's subdomain.

send(connectionName, methodName, arg1, ...argn)
> Invokes a method on a remote *LocalConnection* object.

Event Handlers

allowDomain(domain)
> Callback triggered whenever a message is received. It should return true to permit a cross-domain connection attempt.

onStatus(infoObject)

Callback indicating initial status of a *send()* invocation, where *infoObject*'s level property indicates the status ("status" or "error").

Math Object Flash 5; can be used when exporting Flash 4 movies

access to mathematical functions and constants

```
Math.propertyName
Math.methodName( )
```

The *Math* object provides access to built-in mathematical functions (accessed through methods) and constant values (accessed through properties). There is no *Math()* constructor, and functions like *Math.sin()* are simply functions, not methods that operate on an object.

Properties

E

The constant *e*, the base of natural logarithms, approximately 2.71828.

LN10

The natural logarithm of 10 ($\log_e 10$), approximately 2.30259.

LN2

The natural logarithm of 2 ($\log_e 2$), approximately 0.69315.

LOG10E

The base-10 logarithm of *e*, approximately 0.43429.

LOG2E

The base-2 logarithm of *e*, approximately 1.44270.

PI

The constant π—the ratio of a circle's circumference to its diameter—approximately 3.14159.

SQRT1_2

1 divided by the square root of 2, approximately 0.70711.

SQRT2

The square root of 2, approximately 1.41421.

Methods

abs(x)

    Returns the absolute value of *x*.

acos(x)

    Returns the inverse cosine of a number between −1.0 and 1.0 (result is between 0 and π radians).

asin(x)

    Returns the inverse sine of a number between −1.0 and 1.0 (result is between $-\pi/2$ and $\pi/2$ radians).

atan(x)

    Returns the inverse tangent of a number between −Infinity and Infinity (inclusive). The result is between $-\pi/2$ and $\pi/2$ radians.

atan2(y, x)

    Returns a value between $-\pi$ and π radians that specifies the counterclockwise angle between the positive X-axis and the point (x, y). Note the order of the arguments to this function.

ceil(x)

    Returns *x* rounded up to the next integer.

cos(theta)

    Returns the cosine of the angle *theta*, expressed in radians (result is between −1.0 and 1.0).

exp(x)

    Raises *e* to the power *x*.

floor(x)

    Returns the closest integer less than or equal to *x*.

log(x)

    Computes the natural logarithm of a positive integer.

max(number1, number2)

    Returns the larger of two numbers. It does not support more than two arguments (as JavaScript does).

min(number1, number2)

    Returns the smaller of two numbers. It does not support more than two arguments (as JavaScript does).

pow(base, exponent)
> Raises a number (*base*) to the specified power (*exponent*).

random()
> Retrieves a random floating-point number greater than or equal to 0.0 and less than 1.0.

round(x)
> Calculates the closest integer to *x*.

sin(theta)
> Returns the sine of the angle *theta*, expressed in radians (result is between –1.0 and 1.0).

sqrt(x)
> Returns the square root of a nonnegative number.

tan(theta)
> Returns the tangent of the angle *theta*, expressed in radians (result is between –Infinity and Infinity, inclusive).

maxscroll Property　　　　Flash 4; replaced by TextField.maxscroll in Flash 6

the last legal top line of a text field

```
maxscroll
```

Mouse Object　　　　Flash 5; enhanced in Flash 6 to add listener events

mouse events and control over mouse pointer visibility

```
Mouse.methodName( )
```

The *Mouse* object provides feedback from mouse events and control over the visibility of the mouse pointer. Use the properties _level0._xmouse and _level0._ymouse to determine the mouse pointer's location relative to the Stage of the base movie in the Flash Player.

Methods

addListener(listener)
> Registers an object to receive *onMouseDown()*, *onMouseMove()*, and *onMouseUp()* events.

hide()
> Hides the mouse pointer.

removeListener(listener)
> Cancels event notices for the specified listener.

show()
> Enables (shows) the mouse pointer.

Listener Events

onMouseDown()
> Occurs when the primary mouse button is depressed.

onMouseMove()
> Occurs when the mouse pointer moves.

onMouseUp()
> Occurs when the primary mouse button is released.

See Also *MovieClip.onMouseDown()*, *MovieClip.onMouseMove()*, *MovieClip.onMouseUp()*, `MovieClip._xmouse`, `MovieClip._ymouse`, *updateAfterEvent()*

MovieClip Class   Flash 3; enhanced in Flash 4, Flash 5, and Flash 6

class-like datatype for main movies and movie clips

Constructor

```
new MovieClip();
```

The constructor syntax is used only to create *MovieClip* subclasses. To create a movie clip instance, use *attachMovie()*, *createEmptyMovieClip()*, or *duplicateMovieClip()*. *MovieClip* symbols, on which instances are based, must be created manually in the Flash authoring tool.

Description

MovieClip is a class and also a unique ActionScript datatype used to represent information about, and allow control of, movies and movie clips. For details, see "Using Movie Clips."

The position of a clip is measured in reference to one representative point, its so-called *registration point*, as marked by a crosshair

---

in the clip's Library symbol. Flash's coordinate system inverts the Y-axis of Cartesian coordinates; that is, y values increase in a downward direction, not upward.

As of Flash 6, movie clip instances can respond to events exactly like buttons do. Once a button handler, such as *onPress()*, is defined for a movie clip, the following button-related properties become active: enabled, hitArea, trackAsMenu, and useHandCursor. To provide button-style Up, Over, and Down states for a movie clip, create frames with the special labels _up, _over, and _down. To define the button-style Hit state for a movie clip, use the hitArea property.

Properties

Table 21 lists the properties of the *MovieClip* class. Movie clip properties can be accessed for any movie clip instance and, in most cases, on the main movie timeline (_root). All properties of the current timeline can be accessed without an explicit reference to it, as in _alpha versus *someClip.*_alpha.

Table 21. Movie clip property summary

Property name	Access	Type	Description
_alpha	R/W	number	Opacity percentage: 0 is transparent, 100 is opaque
_currentframe	RO	number	Frame number at which the playhead resides
_droptarget	RO	string	Target path of the clip over which a dragged clip hovers or has been dropped, in slash notation
enabled	R/W	Boolean	Allows or disallows button interaction
focusEnabled	R/W	Boolean	Allows the clip to receive keyboard focus programmatically
_focusrect	R/W	Boolean	Disables automatic yellow rectangle around focused movie clips
_framesloaded	RO	number	Number of frames that have been downloaded
_height	R/W	number	Height, in pixels, of the clip's contents
hitArea	R/W	string	Assigns the clickable area for a button-enabled movie clip

Table 21. Movie clip property summary (continued)

Property name	Access	Type	Description
_name	R/W	string	Identifier of an instance as a string (not a reference)
_parent	RO	MovieClip reference	A reference to the instance or movie (host clip) that contains the current instance
_rotation	R/W	number	Degrees of rotation
tabChildren	R/W	Boolean	Controls whether contained objects are included in the automatic tab order
tabEnabled	R/W	Boolean	Includes or excludes the movie clip from the current tab order
tabIndex	R/W	Boolean	Specifies the movie clip's index in the custom tab order
_target	RO	string	Target path in absolute terms, in slash notation
_totalframes	RO	number	Number of frames in the movie or clip's timeline
trackAsMenu	R/W	Boolean	Modifies the *onRelease( )* handler requirements, enabling menu-style behavior
_url	RO	string	Disk or network location of the source *.swf* file
useHandCursor	R/W	Boolean	Dictates whether a hand cursor is displayed when the mouse is over the clip (applies to clips with button handlers only)
_visible	R/W	Boolean	Visibility: true if shown, false if hidden
_width	R/W	number	Width, in pixels, of the clip's current contents
_x	R/W	number	Horizontal location of movie clip, in pixels
_xmouse	RO	number	Horizontal location of mouse pointer, in pixels
_xscale	R/W	number	Horizontal scaling percentage (100 is default)
_y	R/W	number	Vertical location of movie clip, in pixels
_ymouse	RO	number	Vertical location of mouse pointer, in pixels
_yscale	R/W	number	Vertical scaling percentage (100 is default)

Methods

Movie clip methods can be invoked on any movie clip instance and, in most cases, on the main movie timeline (_root).

attachMovie(symbolID, newName, depth, initObj)
> Creates a new instance based on an exported symbol from the current document's Library, and optionally assigns the instance properties attached to an initialization object (*initObj*).

beginFill(RGB, alpha)
> Starts drawing a solid-filled shape.

beginGradientFill(fillType, colors, alphas, ratios, matrix)
> Starts drawing a gradient-filled shape.

clear()
> Erases all runtime-created drawings from a movie clip.

createEmptyMovieClip(instanceName, depth)
> Creates a new, empty *MovieClip* instance.

createTextField((instanceName, depth, x, y, w, h)
> Creates a new *TextField* object.

curveTo(ctrlX, ctrlY, anchorX, anchorY)
> Draws a curved line using a quadratic Bézier curve.

duplicateMovieClip(newName, depth, initObj)
> Creates a copy of a movie clip instance, and optionally assigns the instance properties attached to an initialization object (*initObj*).

endFill()
> Terminates the fill begun with *beginFill()* or *beginGradientFill()*.

getBounds(movieClip)
> Returns an object whose properties (xMin, xMax, yMin, and yMax) give the clip's bounding box.

getBytesLoaded()
> Returns the number of downloaded bytes of an instance or a movie (not applicable to author-time clips).

getBytesTotal()
> Returns the physical byte size of an instance or a main movie.

---

getDepth()

Returns the movie clip's position in the visual content stack.

getURL(url, window, method)

Loads an external document (usually a web page) into the browser window. The optional *method* is "GET" or "POST".

globalToLocal(pointObj)

Converts a point—specified as x and y properties of an object—from Stage coordinates to instance coordinates.

gotoAndPlay(frameNumberOrLabel)

Moves the playhead of an instance or movie to a specific frame and then plays the instance or movie.

gotoAndStop(frameNumberOrLabel)

Moves the playhead of an instance or movie to a specific frame and then stops the playhead.

hitTest(x, y, shapeFlag) or hitTest(target)

Returns a Boolean indicating whether a clip intersects with a given point or another clip.

lineStyle(thickness, RGB, alpha)

Sets stroke thickness, color, and transparency for the *lineTo()* and *curveTo()* methods.

lineTo(x, y)

Draws a straight line from current pen location to the specified point.

loadMovie(url, method)

Loads an external *.swf* or *.jpg* file into the Player. The optional *method* is "GET" or "POST".

loadVariables(url, method)

Retrieves external data composed of variable names and values, and converts that data into equivalent movie clip timeline variables. The optional *method* is "GET" or "POST".

localToGlobal(pointObj)

Converts a point—specified as x and y properties of an object—from instance coordinates to Stage coordinates.

moveTo(x, y)

Moves the drawing pen to a new position without drawing a line.

nextFrame()

> Moves the playhead of a clip instance or the main movie ahead one frame and stops it there.

play()

> Starts the playhead of a clip instance or the main movie in motion (i.e., plays the clip).

prevFrame()

> Moves the playhead of a clip instance or the main movie back one frame and stops it there.

removeMovieClip()

> Deletes a runtime-created movie clip instance.

setMask(maskMovieClip)

> Assigns a movie clip as a mask for another clip.

startDrag() or startDrag(lockCenter, l, t, r, b)

> Causes an instance or movie to follow the mouse pointer physically within optional constraints.

stop()

> Pauses the playhead of a clip instance or the main movie. Flash continues to render graphics and detect events even while the playhead is stopped.

stopDrag()

> Ends any drag operation in progress.

swapDepths(target) or swapDepths(depth)

> Alters the graphic layering of an instance in the visual content stack.

unloadMovie()

> Removes a clip instance or main movie from a document level or host clip.

valueOf()

> Returns an object reference to the instance.

Events

As of Flash 6, *Button* events (e.g., *onPress()*, *onRelease()*, and *onRollOver()*) are also available for movie clips, although not for main movie timelines (_root). Movie clip event handlers can be created in the following ways:

- By attaching an *onClipEvent()* block directly to a movie clip instance at authoring time
- By attaching a button-style *on()* block directly to a movie clip instance at authoring time
- By assigning a callback function to the associated event property with ActionScript

The supported movie clip event handlers are listed in Table 22. All the event handlers in the table are new in Flash 6, but the Flash 5 equivalents are shown where applicable. With the exception of *onKillFocus()* and *onSetFocus()*, events listed without Flash 5 equivalents are adopted *Button* events.

Table 22. Movie clip event handler summary

Clip event handler	Clip event occurs when...	Flash 5 equivalent
onData( )	The clip receives the end of a stream of loaded variables, or a portion of a loaded movie	onClipEvent(data)
onDragOut( )	The mouse is pressed over the clip, then moves off the clip before the mouse is released	None; on(dragOut) supported in Flash 6
onDragOver( )	The mouse is pressed over the clip, then moves off and back onto the clip	None; on(dragOver) supported in Flash 6
onEnterFrame( )	One tick of the frame rate passes in the Flash Player	onClipEvent(enter-Frame)
onKeyDown( )	A key is depressed while the clip is on stage and has keyboard focus	onClipEvent(key-Down)
onKeyUp( )	A depressed key is released while the clip is on stage and has keyboard focus	onClipEvent(keyUp)
onKillFocus(newFocus)	The clip loses keyboard focus	None
onLoad( )	The clip first appears on stage, or a *.swf* file finishes loading into the clip	onClipEvent(load)
onMouseDown( )	Primary mouse button is depressed (anywhere over the movie) while the clip is on stage	onClipEvent(mouse-Down)
onMouseMove( )	Mouse pointer moves (even a teensy bit) while the clip is on stage	onClipEvent(mouse-Move)

Table 22. Movie clip event handler summary (continued)

Clip event handler	Clip event occurs when...	Flash 5 equivalent
onMouseUp( )	Primary mouse button is depressed (anywhere over the movie) and released while the clip is on stage	onClipEvent(mouse-Up)
onPress( )	The mouse is pressed over the clip	None; on(press) supported in Flash 6
onRelease( )	The mouse is pressed and then released over the clip	None; on(release) supported in Flash 6
onReleaseOutside( )	The mouse is pressed over the clip and then released after moving off the clip	None; on(releaseOutside) supported in Flash 6
onRollOut( )	The mouse pointer moves off the clip while the mouse button is not depressed	None; on(rollOut) supported in Flash 6
onRollOver( )	The mouse pointer moves over the clip while the mouse button is not depressed	None; on(rollOver) supported in Flash 6
onSetFocus(*oldFocus*)	The clip gains keyboard focus	None
onUnload( )	The clip is removed from the Stage or *unloadMovie( )* executes	onClipEvent(unload)

NaN
Flash 5

constant representing invalid numeric data (Not-a-Number)
read-only

NaN

new Operator
Flash 5

create and return an instance of the class specified by Constructor

new *Constructor*( )

newline Constant
Flash 4

insert a line break

newline

The constant newline represents a standard line break character
(ASCII 10) and is used to force a line break in a block of text

(usually for display in a text field). Within a string, you can also use "\n" to force a line break.

nextFrame( ) Flash 2

advance a movie or movie clip's playhead one frame and stop it

```
nextFrame( )
```

nextScene( ) Flash 2

advance a movie's playhead to frame 1 of the next scene

```
nextScene( )
```

Number( ) Flash 5

convert a value to the Number datatype (see Table 4)

```
Number(value)
```

Number Class Flash 5

wrapper class for primitive numeric data

Constructor

```
new Number(value)
```

Description

The *Number* class allows access to built-in properties that represent special numeric values. The *Number.toString()* method can convert between different number systems, such as base-10 (decimal) and base-16 (hexadecimal).

Class Properties

The following properties are accessed directly as properties of the *Number* class, using Number.*propertyName*.

MAX_VALUE
> The largest representable positive number in ActionScript (1.79769313486231e+308).

MIN_VALUE
> The smallest representable positive number in ActionScript (4.94065645841247e-324).

NaN
> Synonymous with global `NaN` property.

NEGATIVE_INFINITY
> Synonymous with `−Infinity`.

POSITIVE_INFINITY
> Synonymous with `Infinity`.

Methods

toString(radix)
> Converts a number (in an optional radix) to a string.

Object Class   Flash 5

the basis for all other classes and generic objects

Constructor

```
new Object()
```

Description

The *Object* class is the base class of the ActionScript object model. *Object* is used as a constructor to create new, generic objects (to which you can attach properties), and as a superclass upon which to base new classes. Some developers also use an object's __proto__ property to establish inheritance between a subclass and its superclass.

To create a generic object of the *Object* class directly, without using a constructor, use an *object literal*—a series of comma-separated property name/value pairs, enclosed in curly braces, such as:

```
{ property1: value1,
  property2: value2, property3: value3 }
```

Properties

constructor
> A reference to the class constructor function used to create the object.

_ _proto_ _

A reference to the prototype property of the object's constructor function. Note the two underscores on either side of the _ _proto_ _ property.

Class Methods

The following method is invoked through the *Object* class itself, not through an instance of the *Object* class.

registerClass(symbolID, theClass)

Assigns a constructor for a movie clip symbol. Used to create a movie clip subclass for components.

Methods

The following are instance-level methods of the *Object* class.

addProperty(propertyName, getterFunction, setterFunction)

Defines a getter/setter property for an object or class.

hasOwnProperty(propName)

Returns true if the specified property is defined directly on an object.

toString()

Returns the value of the object as a string.

unWatch(propName)

Removes an existing watchpoint.

valueOf()

Returns the primitive value of the object.

watch(propName, callback, userData)

Creates a watchpoint to filter property assignment. Flash passes *propName*, *oldval*, *newval*, and *userData* to the *callback* function, which is called whenever the property would otherwise change value. Not all properties can be watched.

parseFloat( )   Flash 5

extract a floating-point number from a string

parseFloat(*stringExpression*)

parseInt( )

Flash 5

extract an integer from a string, or convert numbers to base-10

```
parseInt(stringExpression, radix)
```

The *parseInt()* function converts a string expression to a base-10 integer. It works only with strings that contain a valid string representation of an integer using the specified *radix*. The *radix* defaults to 10 unless *stringExpression* includes a leading zero, which indicates an octal number, or a leading "0x", which indicates a hexadecimal number.

play( )

Flash 2

begin the sequential display of frames in the current timeline (i.e., play the movie)

```
play()
```

prevFrame( )

Flash 2

send a movie's playhead back one frame and stop it there

```
prevFrame()
```

prevScene( )

Flash 2

send a movie's playhead to frame 1 of the previous scene

```
prevScene()
```

print( )

Flash 5

print the frames of a movie or movie clip using vectors

```
print(target, boundingBox)
```

The *print()* function can print the contents of one or more frames of a movie. By default, *print()* prints all of the frames of *target*'s timeline, one frame per page, cropped or scaled according to the *boundingBox* argument, which can be either "bframe" (scale each frame to fit the page), "bmax" (scale each frame relative to all frames), or "bmovie" (scale each frame relative to the frame labeled #b). To designate specific frames for printing (while excluding undesignated frames), assign the label #p to the desired frames.

The *print()* function sends vectors directly to PostScript printers, and sends vectors converted to bitmaps to non-PostScript printers. It cannot be used to print movies with alpha transparency or color transformations (use *printAsBitmap()* instead).

printAsBitmap( )

print the frames of a movie or movie clip as bitmaps

```
printAsBitmap(target, boundingBox)
```

printAsBitmapNum( )

Flash 5

print the frames of a document level as bitmaps

```
printAsBitmapNum(levelNum, boundingBox)
```

printNum( )

Flash 5

print the frames of a document level using vectors

```
printNum(levelNum, boundingBox)
```

_quality

Flash 5

the rendering quality of the Player   read/write

```
_quality
```

The _quality property stores a string that dictates the rendering quality of the Flash Player: "LOW", "AUTOLOW", "MEDIUM", "AUTOHIGH", "HIGH", or "BEST".

See Also   _highQuality, *toggleHighQuality()*

random( )   Flash 4; deprecated in Flash 5 in favor of Math.random( )

generate a random number from 0 to num − 1

```
random(num)
```

removeMovieClip( )

Flash 4

delete a movie clip created at runtime from the Flash Player

```
removeMovieClip(target)
```

_root
Flash 5 (same as "/" in Flash 4 movies)

a reference to the main timeline of the movie in the current level   read-only

```
_root
```

scroll Property
Flash 4; replaced by TextField.scroll in Flash 6

the current top line displayed in a text field

```
scroll
```

Selection Object
Flash 5; enhanced in Flash 6

control over text field selections and movie input focus

```
Selection.methodName( )
```

The *Selection* object is used to control user interaction with text fields, to capture portions of text fields, and to detect keyboard input focus for buttons, movie clips, and text fields. *Selection* is a predefined object, not a class, so its methods are accessed directly, as in:

```
Selection.setFocus(input_txt);
```

Character-manipulation methods of the *Selection* object always refer implicitly to the text field with keyboard focus. Positions of the characters in a text field are referred to with zero-relative indexes.

Methods

addListener(listener)
  Registers an object to receive *onSetFocus( )* event notices.

getBeginIndex( )
  Returns the index of the first selected character in the text field with keyboard focus.

getCaretIndex( )
  Returns the index of the insertion point in a text field.

getEndIndex( )
  Returns the index of the character following the selection in a text field.

getFocus( )

Returns a string identifying the text field, button, or movie clip that is currently focused (or null if none). Use *eval( )* to convert the return value to an identifier.

removeListener(listener)

Cancels event notices for the specified listener.

setFocus(instanceName)

Assigns input focus to a text field, button, or movie clip object.

setSelection(beginIndex, endIndex)

Selects characters from *beginIndex* to *endIndex-1* in the currently focused text field.

Listener Events

onSetFocus(oldFocus, newFocus)

Occurs when input focus changes (use it to trap focus changes globally).

See Also   *TextField.replaceSel( )*

setInterval( )   Flash 6

execute a function or method periodically

```
setInterval(function, interval, arg1, ...argn)
setInterval(object, method, interval, arg1, ...argn)
```

The *setInterval( )* function starts an *interval*, which executes the specified *function* (which must be a function object) or *method* (which must be a string) every *interval* milliseconds. It returns an *interval identifier*, which is used to stop the timed execution using *clearInterval( )*. Arbitrary data can be passed to *function* or *method* via *arg1, ...argn*.

See Also   *clearInterval( )*, the *Date* class, *getTimer( )*, *MovieClip.onEnterFrame( )*

setProperty( )   Flash 4

assign a value to a movie clip property

```
setProperty(movieClip, property, value)
```

local data storage and remote data transmission

Constructor

None; instances are created with *SharedObject.getLocal()* or *SharedObject.getRemote()*.

Description

The *SharedObject* class provides tools for storing ActionScript data on the end user's computer and transferring data between Flash clients via Comm Server.

Local shared objects (LSOs) are more flexible than JavaScript cookies. They allow typed data to be stored and accessed directly through object properties rather than through an awkward cookie string of name/value pairs. Specifically, *SharedObject*s support the following datatypes: *number*, *string*, *boolean*, *undefined*, *null*, *array*, and *object* (custom classes subclassed from *Object* plus the *XML* and *Date* classes). Other built-in ActionScript classes and objects (such as *MovieClip* and *Function*) cannot be stored in a *SharedObject*.

The following code retrieves a local *SharedObject* named "game-Data". It then assigns a property, player1score, and saves the object by invoking *flush()*:

```
// Create/retrieve the SharedObject.
gameData_so = SharedObject.getLocal("gameData");
// Make a property to save.
gameData_so.data.player1score = 2600;
// Attempt to save the SharedObject.
gameData_so.flush();
```

Information on *remote shared objects* (RSOs) can be found in the Comm Server documentation at *http://www.macromedia.com/software/flashcom/*.

Properties

data

Container for the *SharedObject*'s data. For a value to be saved in a shared object, it must be stored within a property of data.

Class Methods

getLocal(objectName, localPath)

Returns a reference to a specified local *SharedObject* instance, optionally specifying the local path.

getRemote(objectName, URI, persistence)

Returns a reference to a remote *SharedObject* instance managed by Comm Server.

Methods

close( )

Closes the connection between a remote shared object and Comm Server.

connect(RMTPConnection)

Connects to a remote shared object on Comm Server.

flush(minimumDiskSpace)

Forces data to be written to disk, and optionally requests approval from the user for more disk space.

getSize( )

Returns the size of the *SharedObject*, in bytes.

setFPS(updatesPerSecond)

Sets the frequency with which changes to a remote shared object are sent to Comm Server.

Event Handlers

onStatus(infoObject)

Invoked when a *SharedObject* generates a status message (e.g., an error, information, or a warning) as contained in the code and level properties of *infoObject*.

Sound Class

Flash 5; enhanced in Flash 6

control over sounds in a movie and external sound loading tools

Constructor

new Sound(*target*)

Description

Objects of the *Sound* class are used to load external sounds and to control both sounds placed at authoring time and sounds loaded at runtime. To create a *Sound* object that controls all the sounds in the Player (including sounds in *.swf* files on document levels), use the *Sound* constructor without any parameters. To create a *Sound* object that controls all the sounds in a particular clip, supply a *target* parameter indicating the clip to control.

Properties

duration
> The total length of the sound, in milliseconds.

id3
> Returns the ID3 tags of an MP3 file as an object with the properties album, artist, comment, genre, songname, track, and year. Available only for sounds that have fully loaded.

position
> The length of time the sound has played, in milliseconds.

Methods

attachSound(linkageIdentifier)
> Associates a sound from the Library with a *Sound* instance.

getBytesLoaded( )
> Returns the number of downloaded bytes of an external sound file.

getBytesTotal( )
> Returns the physical disk size of an external sound file, in bytes.

getPan( )
> Returns the current pan setting, from −100 (left) to 100 (right).

getTransform( )
> Returns an object whose properties (ll, lr, rl, and rr) indicate the current distribution of the channels of a sound to the left and right speakers (i.e., balance).

getVolume( )
> Returns the current volume, usually in the range 0 to 100.

loadSound(url, isStreaming)
> Downloads an external sound file into the Player. When *isStreaming* is true, the sound streams and starts playing automatically; otherwise the sound must be played manually with *start( )*.

setPan(pan)
> Sets the pan across a sound's left and right channels from −100 (left) to 100 (right).

setTransform(tranformObject)
> Distributes the left and right channels between the left and right speakers (i.e., balance) using an object whose properties (ll, lr, rl, and rr) range from 0 to 100 and indicate the current distribution.

setVolume(volume)
> Sets the sound volume, usually from 0 to 100.

start(secondOffset, loops)
> Starts playing an attached or loaded event sound.

stop(linkageIdentifier)
> Silences all sounds, or a specified attached or loaded sound.

Event Handlers

onLoad(success)
> Occurs when an external sound finishes loading. The Boolean *success* indicates whether the load succeeded.

onSoundComplete( )
> Occurs when a sound finishes playing.

_soundbuftime   Flash 4

length of a streaming sound, in seconds, to preload (default is 5)   read/write

_soundbuftime

access to a movie's size, scale settings, and alignment

```
Stage.propertyName
Stage.methodName()
```

The *Stage* object represents the characteristics of the Flash Player's runtime display area. Note that *Stage* is a predefined object, not a class.

Properties

align

Alignment of the movie in the Flash Player, such as "" (empty string for centered), "B", "T", "L", "LB", "LT", "R", "RB", "RT".

height

Pixel height of the available Flash Player display area or the author-time document height, depending on the value of scaleMode.

scaleMode

Dictates how the movie is sized, relative to the Player ("exactFit", "showAll", "noBorder", or "noScale").

showMenu

Boolean; determines the items displayed in the Flash Player's contextual menu (if true, displays all items; if false, displays short menu).

width

Pixel width of the available Flash Player display area or the author-time document width, depending on the value of scaleMode.

Methods

addListener(listener)

Registers an object to receive *onResize()* events.

removeListener(listener)

Cancels event notices for the specified listener.

Listener Events

onResize()
  Occurs when the movie is resized.

startDrag( ) Flash 4

begin dragging a movie clip with optional constraints

```
startDrag(target)
startDrag(target, lockCenter)
startDrag(target, lockCenter, l, t, r, b)
```

stop( ) Flash 2

pause the current timeline's playhead at the current frame

```
stop()
```

stopAllSounds( ) Flash 3

silence currently playing sounds

```
stopAllSounds()
```

stopDrag( ) Flash 4

end any movie clip drag operation in progress

```
stopDrag()
```

#strict Pragma Flash 5 (undocumented)

activate enhanced conformance to ECMA-262 standard

```
#strict
```

An undocumented and volatile feature, the #strict pragma forces
the Flash Player to conform more closely to the ECMA-262 specification, upon which ActionScript is based. The #strict pragma is
known to crash Internet Explorer on Windows under Flash Player
6, and therefore should not be used.

String( )

convert a value to the string datatype (see Table 5)

```
String(value)
```

String Class

wrapper class for string primitive type

Constructor

```
new String(value)
```

Description

The *String* class performs string-related operations, such as searching strings and extracting substrings. It is also used to access the *fromCharCode()* class method to create a new string based on specified Unicode code points.

Properties

length
    Returns the number of characters in a string.

Class Methods

The following method is invoked through the *String* class itself, not through an instance of the *String* class:

fromCharCode(code_point1, ...code_pointn)
    Generates a string from one or more Unicode code points.

Methods

The following object methods are invoked through an instance of the *String* class:

charAt(index)
    Retrieves a character at a specific (zero-relative) position in the string.

charCodeAt(index)
    Retrieves the code point of a character at a specific (zero-relative) position in the string.

concat(value1, value2, ...valuen)

Combines one or more items into a single string.

indexOf(substring, startIndex)

Finds the first occurrence of a specified substring in a string starting at the optional offset.

lastIndexOf(substring, startIndex)

Finds the last occurrence of a specified substring in a string starting at the optional offset.

slice(startIndex, endIndex)

Extracts a substring from a string, based on positive or negative character positions.

split(delimiter)

Converts a string to an array by breaking it into elements demarcated by *delimiter*.

substr(startIndex, length)

Extracts a substring from a string, based on a starting position and length.

substring(startIndex, endIndex)

Extracts a substring from a string, based on positive character positions only.

toLowerCase( )

Returns a lowercase version of a string.

toUpperCase( )

Returns an uppercase version of a string.

super "Operator"   Flash 6

invoke a superclass's constructor or overridden method

```
super(arg1, arg2,...argn)
super.methodName(arg1, arg2,...argn)
```

System Object   Flash 6

access to Player and system settings and specifications

```
System.propertyName
System.methodName()
```

The *System* object provides information about, and control over, features of the Flash Player and the system on which it is running. The *Capabilities* object is documented earlier as the *Capabilities Object* (under "C"). The *Security* object's single method is documented under *System.security.allowDomain()*.

Properties

capabilities
    A reference to the *Capabilities* object.

security
    Object for setting cross-domain movie permissions.

useCodepage
    If true, forces the Flash Player to use the operating system's code page rather than Unicode. (Not recommended when Unicode is available!)

Methods

showSettings(tabID)
    Displays one of the tabs of the Flash Player Settings dialog box: Privacy (0), Local Storage (1), Microphone (2), or Camera (3).

System.security.allowDomain( ) Method   Flash 6

sets cross-domain movie permissions

```
System.security.allowDomain(domain1,...domainn)
```

The *allowDomain()* method allows movies at other domains to perform restricted operations on the current movie. For details, see "Security Restrictions."

targetPath( )   Flash 5

returns the absolute path to a movie or movie clip, in dot notation

```
targetPath (movieOrMovieClip)
```

tellTarget( ) "Tell Target" in Flash 3; deprecated in Flash 5

execute statements in the scope of a remote movie clip

```
tellTarget (target) {
  statements
}
```

TextField Class Flash 6

display and manipulate text on screen

Constructor

None. *TextField* objects are created manually in the authoring tool or programmatically via the *MovieClip.createTextField( )* method.

Description

The *TextField* class provides control over text displayed on screen. In order to gain access to a *TextField* instance for a field created at authoring time, we must set its type to Dynamic Text or Input Text and assign it an instance name via the Property inspector. To format the appearance of text in a text field, use either a *TextFormat* object or the *TextField*.html property.

Properties

_alpha
    Opacity percentage: 0 is transparent, 100 is opaque.

autoSize
    Matches the text field's bounding rectangle size to its text. The four possible values are "none" (the default), "left", "right", and "center".

background
    Boolean; turns text field background on and off.

backgroundColor
    RGB number specifying the text field's background color.

border
    Boolean; turns the text field border on and off.

borderColor
    RGB number specifying the text field's border color.

TextField Class | 119

bottomScroll
> The one-relative index of the text field's lowest visible line.

condenseWhite
> Boolean; specifies whether whitespace in HTML text should be condensed.

embedFonts
> Boolean; if true, Flash renders text using fonts exported with the movie; otherwise, it uses system fonts.

_height
> Height of the text field's bounding box, in pixels.

hscroll
> Horizontal scroll position of the text field, in pixels.

html
> Boolean; enables or disables HTML display.

htmlText
> HTML source code to render in the text field.

length
> The number of characters in the text field.

maxChars
> Limits the allowed length of user input.

maxhscroll
> The farthest position text can be scrolled to the left.

maxscroll
> The last legal top line of a text field.

multiline
> Boolean; enables or disables multiple-line user input.

_name
> The instance name of the *TextField* object.

_parent
> A reference to the movie clip in which the text field resides.

password
> Boolean; if true, Flash obscures characters displayed in the field (not truly secure).

---

restrict
> Limits text entry to the specified characters.

_rotation
> Rotation of the text field, in degrees.

scroll
> The current top line displayed in the text field.

selectable
> Boolean; enables or disables selection by the user.

tabEnabled
> Boolean; includes or excludes the text field from the current tab order.

tabIndex
> Specifies the text field's index in the custom tab order.

_target
> The target path of the text field, in slash syntax.

text
> Specifies the characters to be rendered in the field.

textColor
> Sets the color for all characters in the text field.

textHeight
> Pixel height of all the text in the text field.

textWidth
> Pixel width of the longest line in the text field.

type
> Specifies whether the field can accept user input (if type is "input"). Dynamic fields (type "dynamic") cannot accept user input but can be controlled via ActionScript. Text fields created via *MovieClip.createTextField()* default to type "dynamic". Static text (the authoring tool default) cannot accept user input or be controlled via ActionScript.

_url
> The network URL of the movie clip that contains the field.

variable
> Associates a variable with the text field's text property, for Flash 5 backward compatibility only.

_visible
>   Boolean; whether the text field is shown or hidden.

_width
>   Width of the text field's bounding box, in pixels.

wordWrap
>   Boolean; enables or disables automatic line breaking for long lines.

_x
>   Horizontal location of the text field, in pixels.

_xmouse
>   Horizontal location of the mouse pointer, in pixels, relative to the text field's left edge.

_xscale
>   Width of the text field, as a percentage of original.

_y
>   Vertical location of the text field, in pixels.

_ymouse
>   Vertical location of the mouse pointer, in pixels, relative to the text field's top edge.

_yscale
>   Height of the text field, as a percentage of original.

Class Methods

getFontList()
>   Returns the fonts installed on the user's system, as an array of strings.

Methods

addListener(listener)
>   Registers an object to receive onChanged() and onScroller() events.

getDepth()
>   Returns the position of the text field in the parent clip's visual content stack.

---

getNewTextFormat( )
  Retrieves the default *TextFormat* object for the text field, which controls the formatting of any text added to the field.

getTextFormat(beginIndex, endIndex)
  Retrieves a *TextFormat* object describing the formatting for existing text (for the entire field or for an optional character span).

removeListener(listener)
  Cancels event notices for the specified listener.

removeTextField( )
  Deletes a runtime-created text field.

replaceSel(newText)
  Replaces selected text (without disturbing formatting).

setNewTextFormat(textFormatObject)
  Sets the default formatting for newly created text in the text field using an instance of the *TextFormat* class.

setTextFormat(beginIndex, endIndex, textFormatObject)
  Sets the formatting of specified characters using an instance of the *TextFormat* class. If you specify the optional *endIndex*, you must also specify *beginIndex*.

Event Handlers

onChanged(changedField)
  Callback invoked when user input is detected.

onKillFocus(newFocus)
  Callback invoked when the field loses focus.

onScroller(scrolledField)
  Callback invoked when any scroll property changes.

onSetFocus(oldFocus)
  Callback invoked when the field gains focus.

Listener Events

onChanged(changedField)
  Occurs when user input is detected.

onScroller(scrolledField)
  Occurs when any scroll property changes.

retrieve or set a text field's visual formatting

Constructor

```
new TextFormat()
new TextFormat(font, size, color, bold, italic, underline,
url, target, align, leftMargin, rightMargin, indent, leading)
```

Description

A *TextFormat* object's properties control the display attributes of
a specific character or, alternatively, report the display attributes
common to a series of characters in a *TextField* object.

When text is added to a field, it is formatted according to the field's
default format, accessible via *TextField.getNewTextFormat()*. To
modify a field's default format, create a *TextFormat* object, set its
properties, and pass it to *TextField.setNewTextFormat()*. To format
existing characters in a text field, use *TextField.setTextFormat()*.

Properties

align
> Specifies horizontal paragraph alignment ("left", "right", or
> "center").

blockIndent
> Specifies paragraph indentation from the left edge in pixels.

bold
> Boolean; specifies whether to display characters in bold.

bullet
> Boolean; specifies whether to add bullets to paragraphs.

color
> Specifies character color as a hex RGB triplet, such as
> 0xFF0000.

font
> Sets the font for the specified characters.

indent
> Specifies indentation from the text field's left border, in
> pixels, for a paragraph's first line.

---

italic
> Boolean; specifies whether to display characters in italics.

leading
> Specifies line spacing, in pixels.

leftMargin
> Specifies the margin to the left of a paragraph, in pixels

rightMargin
> Specifies the margin to the right of a paragraph, in pixels.

size
> Specifies character font size, in points.

tabStops
> Specifies horizontal tab stops, in pixels, as an array.

target
> Specifies the window or frame for a hypertext link.

underline
> Boolean; specifies whether to underline displayed characters.

url
> Specifies a hypertext link. Requires `TextField.html` to be set to true to work.

Methods

getTextExtent(text)
> Returns an object with height and width properties giving the pixel dimensions of a string rendered in the format of the text format object.

toggleHighQuality( )   Flash 2; deprecated in Flash 5

switch between High quality and Low quality rendering in the Player

```
toggleHighQuality()
```

trace( )   Flash 4

display a value in the Output window in Test Movie mode (authoring tool only)

```
trace(value)
```

typeof Operator

determine the datatype of an expression or identifier

typeof operand

Returns a string indicating the datatype of operand. One of "string", "number", "boolean", "null", "undefined", "object", "movieclip", or "function".

unescape( )

decode an escaped (URL-encoded) string

unescape(stringExpression)

See Also escape( )

unloadMovie( )

unload a movie or movie clip from the Player

unloadMovie(target)

See Also loadMovie( )

unloadMovieNum( )

remove a movie from a document level, by number

unloadMovieNum(levelNum)

updateAfterEvent( )

render the contents of the Stage between frames

updateAfterEvent()

When a function executes between frames in the Flash Player, any visual changes to the screen are not displayed until the next frame is rendered. However, in the following cases, you can force a screen refresh manually by invoking *updateAfterEvent()* from:

- A *setInterval()* callback function
- A movie clip's *onMouseMove()*, *onMouseDown()*, *onMouseUp()*, *onKeyDown()*, or *onKeyUp()* handlers

$version

the version of the Flash Player

```
_root.$version
```

The $version property returns the same string as the global *getVersion()* function and the System.capabilities.version property but is supported in Flash 4.0.11.0 and later. See the capabilities.version entry for details on its format.

XML Class

DOM-based support for XML-structured data

Constructor

```
new XML(source)
```

Description

We use objects of the *XML* class to manipulate the content of an XML document in an object-oriented manner and to send XML-formatted data to and from Flash. Using the methods and properties of an *XML* object, we can build an XML-structured document (or read an existing one) and access, change, or remove the information in that document.

When constructing a new *XML* object, we can pass in an optional string containing well-formed XML data to be parsed into an XML object hierarchy. The results of a parsing attempt can be determined via the status property, whose possible values are listed in Table 23.

Table 23. XML parsing status codes

Status	Description
0	The document parsed without errors (i.e., success).
−2	A CDATA section was not properly terminated.
−3	The XML declaration was not properly terminated.
−4	The DOCTYPE declaration was not properly terminated.
−5	A comment was not properly terminated.
−6	An XML element was malformed.

Table 23. XML parsing status codes (continued)

Status	Description
−7	Not enough memory to parse the XML source.
−8	An attribute value was not properly terminated.
−9	A start tag had no corresponding end tag.
−10	An end tag had no corresponding start tag.

Properties

attributes
> An object whose properties store element attributes.

childNodes
> An array of references to a node's children.

contentType
> The MIME content type to be transmitted to servers.

docTypeDecl
> The document's DOCTYPE tag.

firstChild
> A reference to the first descendant of a node.

ignoreWhite
> Boolean; indicates whether to ignore whitespace nodes during XML parsing (default is false).

lastChild
> A reference to the last descendant of a node.

loaded
> Boolean; status of the last *load()* or *sendAndLoad()* operation.

nextSibling
> A reference to the node after this node in the current level of the object hierarchy.

nodeName
> The name of the current node (matching the tag name for element nodes, or null for text nodes).

nodeType
> The type of the current node, either 1 (an element node) or 3 (a text node).

nodeValue

The value of the current node, as a string (i.e., the text contained by a text node, or null for element nodes). Unlike *toString()*, nodeValue converts predefined entities to corresponding characters.

parentNode

A reference to the immediate ancestor of a node.

previousSibling

A reference to the node before this node in the current level of the object hierarchy.

status

Numeric error code describing the result of parsing XML source into an object hierarchy. 0 indicates success; negative numbers indicate errors. See Table 23.

xmlDecl

The document's XML declaration tag.

Methods

addRequestHeader (headerName, headerValue)

Specifies a custom HTTP POST header. Added in Flash Player 6.0.65.0.

appendChild(childNode)

Adds a new child node, or moves an existing node.

cloneNode(deep)

Creates a copy of a node (copies child nodes recursively when *deep* is true).

createElement(tagName)

Creates a new element node, which must be inserted in the hierarchy separately.

createTextNode(text)

Creates a new text node, which must be inserted in the hierarchy separately.

getBytesLoaded()

The number of downloaded bytes of an external XML file.

getBytesTotal()

The physical disk size of an external XML file, in bytes.

hasChildNodes( )
> Returns a Boolean indicating whether a node has any descendants.

insertBefore(newChild, beforeChild)
> Adds a sibling node before an existing node.

load(url)
> Imports XML source code from the external file, script, or application at *url*.

parseXML(string)
> Parses a string of XML source code.

removeNode( )
> Deletes a node from an XML object hierarchy.

send(url, windowOrFrameName)
> Sends XML source code to an external script or application and displays the results in a browser window.

sendAndLoad(url, resultXML)
> Sends XML source code to an external script or application and receives XML source code in return.

toString( )
> Converts an *XML* object to a string (unlike nodeValue, *toString( )* does not convert predefined entities to corresponding characters).

Event Handlers

onData(src)
> Handler executed when external XML source code finishes loading (*src* contains the loaded XML source code).

onLoad(success)
> Handler executed when external XML data has been parsed into an object hierarchy. The Boolean *success* indicates whether load succeeded.

XMLnode Class   Flash 5 (undocumented)

internal superclass of the XML class

Technically, every XML object hierarchy includes two kinds of object nodes:

- One *XML* top-level node, which serves as the main container for the hierarchy
- An arbitrary number of *XMLnode* nodes, which are the children of the top-level node

The top-level node is an instance of the *XML* class, which inherits from the *XMLnode* class, so main container nodes have all the properties and methods defined by *XMLnode* in addition to those defined by *XML*. In contrast, the child nodes are actually instances of the *XMLnode* class, not the *XML* class.

The properties, methods, and event handlers available through the *XML* and *XMLNode* classes are listed in Table 24.

Table 24. XMLnode and XML properties, methods, and event handlers

XMLnode and XML	XML only
appendChild( )	contentType
attributes	*createElement( )*
childNodes	*createTextNode( )*
cloneNode( )	docTypeDecl
firstChild	*getBytesTotal( )*
hasChildNodes( )	*getBytesLoaded( )*
insertBefore( )	ignoreWhite
lastChild	*load( )*
nextSibling	loaded
nodeName	*onData( )*
nodeType	*onLoad( )*
nodeValue	*parseXML( )*
parentNode	*send( )*
previousSibling	*sendAndLoad( )*
removeNode( )	status
toString( )	xmlDecl

support for a persistent client/server TCP/IP connection

Constructor

new XMLSocket()

Description

The *XMLSocket* class provides a persistent TCP/IP socket connection to a server application. We use *XMLSocket* connections to develop systems that require frequent server updates, such as a chat room or a networked multiplayer game. *XMLSocket* connections require a custom socket server such as those listed back in Table 11.

Methods

close()
    Terminates an open connection to a server application.

connect(host, port)
    Attempts to establish a new connection to a server application.

send(xmlObject)
    Sends an XML object hierarchy to a server application as a string.

Event Handlers

onClose()
    Executes when the server terminates the connection.

onConnect(success)
    Executes when a connection attempt completes. The Boolean *success* is true if the connection attempt succeeded.

onData(src)
    Executes when data is received but has not yet been parsed as XML.

onXML(xmlObject)
    Executes when data has been received and parsed into an XML object hierarchy.

Index

We'd like to hear your suggestions for improving our indexes. Send email to
index@oreilly.com.